Praise for *Approv...*

"Readers went wild for this Type A comic's ability to write about everything—from struggling with anorexia to the travails of eyelash extensions to her mother's death—with a magic mix of vulnerability and jest."

—*Elle* (Readers' Prize)

"Those wise enough to pick up this collection of essays are about to find their newest best friend in Salie. . . . Plan on reading this once for entertainment, or better, twice for the life lessons available."

—*Booklist*

"Funny, touching essays on being a multifaceted woman with unique dreams, desires, and needs."

—*Kirkus Reviews*

"When Salie . . . writes from the heart, the memoir is as pleasing as they come."

—*Publishers Weekly*

"I absolutely loved this book. And I'm not just saying that because I want Faith Salie to like me."

—Elizabeth Gilbert

"Faith Salie is exquisitely, sometimes painfully, honest and real—and very, very funny. Whether you see where she's coming from or think she's bonkers, you'll be wildly entertained by this book."

—Emily Gould, author of *Friendship*

"I dare you not to fall in love with Faith Salie. Her book is charmingly self-deprecating and snort-soda-through-your-nose laugh inducing! She reveals such vulnerability and insight into our flawed human condition, you'll be both dazzled and deeply moved."

—Annabelle Gurwitch, *New York Times* bestselling author of *I See You Made an Effort*

"I'm going to be an enabler and give Faith Salie some pure, high-grade, unadulterated approval. Because she deserves it. This book is a hilarious and emotional look at love, career, and Faith's mom's pelvic floor (among other things). You will approve of it as well."

—A. J. Jacobs

"If it is a comfort to you, as it is to me, to find that somebody as smart, sophisticated, funny, accomplished, graceful, witty, and (not incidentally) drop-dead gorgeous as Faith Salie is, inside, a weird, sopping mess of crippling insecurities, just like you are— then keep this book close at hand. You will turn to it in times of trouble, stress, and self-doubt. Remember, if a genuine Rhodes Scholar in a size two dress can be this messed up, then you're going to be just fine."

—Peter Sagal, host of NPR's *Wait Wait . . . Don't Tell Me!*

"*Approval Junkie* by Faith Salie is a hilarious cry for help that will leave you thinking, *Oh sh*t, I think I'm an approval junkie too!* (Or maybe that was just me?) Do yourself a favor and read this book and then give it a five-star review, because anything below four might send Faith over the edge."

—Jen Mann, *New York Times* bestselling author of
*People I Want to Punch in the Throat: Competitive Crafters,
Drop-Off Despots, and Other Suburban Scourges*

"I'm not the laugh-out-loud type; I'm the stone-faced-while-everyone-else-is-howling type. Well, I laughed out loud while compulsively reading this hilarious, sometimes, heartbreaking book. Let the Tina Fey comparisons begin!"

—Jancee Dunn, author of
How Not to Hate Your Husband After Kids

"Over the top, all too true, and laugh-out-loud funny, all in one easy-to-approve-of package."

—Seth Godin, author of *Your Turn*

Approval Junkie

My Heartfelt (and Occasionally Inappropriate) Quest to Please Just About Everyone, and Ultimately Myself

Faith Salie

THREE RIVERS PRESS
NEW YORK

Library of Congress Cataloging-in-Publication Data
Salie, Faith, 1971–
Approval junkie / Faith Salie. —First edition.
pages cm
Summary: "In this hilarious collection of essays, comedian Faith Salie
reflects on the absurd hoops she's jumped through in order to win approval.
From running in place in a darkened shower in Africa at 4 am to lose weight,
to agreeing to an exorcism at the behest of her crazy ex-husband, to eating
pig organs with Harrison Ford's son after her producers told her it would
"make good TV," Salie has done it all in the hopes of achieving positive
reinforcement from colleagues, friends, and her aforementioned ex (or as
she calls him, "was-band"). With thoughtfulness and sarcasm, Salie reflects
on why it is she tries so hard to please others, highlighting a phenomenon
that many people—especially women—experience at home and in the work
place. Equal parts laugh-out-loud funny and poignant, Approval Junkie is
a humorous exploration into why it is that we so desperately try to please
others at the expense of our own happiness" —Provided by publisher.
ISBN 978-0-553-41993-1 (hardback) —ISBN 978-0-553-41995-5
(tradepaper) —ISBN 978-0-553-41994-8 (ebook)
1. Salie, Faith, 1971- 2. Actors—United States—Biography.
3. Social acceptance—Humor. I. Title.
PN2287.S265A3 2016
791.4302'8092—dc23
[B]
2015036040

ISBN 978-0-553-41995-5
Ebook ISBN 978-0-553-41994-8

For John,
who reminds me that I am always enough . . .

and

for Augustus and Minerva,
who teach me that I am more than I ever imagined

Contents

Faith Accompli

Fail again. Fail better.
Samuel Beckett

If you've come seeking advice on how not to seek approval, I'm afraid I'll disappoint. I do not have a twelve-step program to alleviate the desire for approbation. However, I can offer you something that's the exact opposite of a cure, because I'd hate for you to leave empty-handed:

12 Steps You Might Take to Win Approval

1. Make good grades.
2. Go to church or pay a lot for High Holidays orchestra seats.
3. Refrain from having sex to be "good"/Be good at having sex.
4. Casually, and only semiaccurately, reference Schrödinger's cat in conversation.
5. Run in place in a dark shower for forty-five minutes at 4 a.m. every morning so you won't gain weight on an African safari.

6. Do things to make your parents proud.

7. Do things to make your therapist proud.

8. Enlist Michael Jackson's choreographer to plan your first wedding dance and a Broadway veteran to choreograph your first *second* wedding dance.

9. Say yes (e.g., "Yes, I'll provide three dozen nut-free kosher cupcakes even though I'm not Jewish!") when you really should say no.

10. Moderate a small, jovial panel discussion as you spend two hours pushing your baby out, so you don't make this whole giving birth thing about you you you, even as your child rips a hole in your labia, forever ruining your chances of going into porn at the age of forty-one.

11. Stay in a relationship with someone whom you're determined to win over.

12. Refrain from ending your sentences in a preposition.

I am an approval junkie. When I told people the name of the book I was writing, some immediately smiled and said, "Great title." No questions asked; they got it. A few looked concerned and said, "Really? I wouldn't have thought that of you." At which point I put down the cake I was frosting for them while simultaneously breastfeeding my daughter and doing squats and explained that I'm not ashamed about wanting approval. It kept my high school GPA very high. It's kept my BMI somewhat low. It's kept me on my toes when I wasn't already wearing heels to elongate my legs.

We all know someone who says, "I got to where I am by not giving a shit." I believe this can be true of psychopaths and Buddhist nuns. But of everyone else, I'm a little admiring and a lot skeptical. How can you not give even a little tiny shit? Kanye West tweets, "I don't give a fuck what people think because people don't think." Then he incites a Twitter war with Jimmy Kimmel after Kimmel has kids read a transcript of Kanye's own words announcing that he is the number one rock star in the world and invented leather jogging pants. On the flip side, we have Sally Field, accepting her Oscar, beaming while crying, ". . . you like me, right now, you like me!" Who's more honest—Yeezus or Gidget?

Famous people I've interviewed—powerful people, brilliant people, people whom you look at and think, *Seriously, do you not have pores?*—have turned to me after interviews and asked, "Was I okay? I hope I was okay." Even Jesus wanted to make his mother happy at the wedding in Cana with that water/wine mindfreak.

Approval may not be your raison d'être, but it never sucks to feel it. It connects you to your audience, which is the human race. Approval makes the world go round even if many of us want to transcend our hunger for it.

Wanting approval is a naked thing. It says *Listen to me, love me, understand me.* Those are vulnerable requests. A junkie keeps requesting.

Being a true approval junkie does not quite equal being a perfectionist. A perfectionist won't try for fear of falling short. An approval junkie stumbles, trips, and falls again, each time taking a bow for trying. A perfectionist won't leave the house without her face on. An approval junkie leaves the house to face the next challenge. She knows no one ever created something applause-worthy—something new or compelling or hilarious—by playing it safe.

While a junkie laps up smiles, it's also too simple to label

her a people pleaser. Pleasing people can feel deeply grati-
fying when it doesn't involve, say, letting someone pee on
you (more on that later, unfortunately). But caring too much
about people liking you will confine you forever to mediocrity and second-guessing yourself and may force you to
engage in meaningful conversation about following one's
dreams with your Uber driver so he'll give you a five-star
rating. One doesn't want to become a short-order cook of a
pleaser, catering to countless individual likes and dislikes.
Nor does one want to sling a bland offering meant to appeal to a mass palate. An approval junkie knows, "You can
please some of the people all of the time and you can please
all of the people some of the time, but you'd have to spend an
awful lot of time figuring out what pleases the people, which
is time you could be spending on getting your candy striper
uniform altered so it fits more flatteringly." I mean, just for
example. Ultimately, an approval junkie desires most to
please her toughest critic, which is herself.

An approval junkie appreciates being noticed but isn't a
wanton attention whore. One craves attention for the *right*
things, like instant improvisational skills or long eyelashes. I
personally do not want attention at any price. For example, I
was never one of those Goth teens (although I played one for
a season on a sitcom that *TV Guide* named number 30 on its
"50 Worst Shows of All Time"). And now—while I'm delighted when people occasionally recognize me on the street
or when I'm buying support hose to fly while bulbously pregnant to interview an NBA player about his unibrow—it's a
double-edged sword. I almost wish they wouldn't recognize
me and would rather murmur to their partner, "Doesn't

that lady who's inexplicably humming show tunes look like a tired version of that gal on *CBS News Sunday Morning*?" Or the kids at the Apple Genius bar who recognize my voice from *Wait Wait . . . Don't Tell Me!*—I feel sad for them that they must be thinking, *She doesn't* <u>*sound*</u> *like someone who wears clogs with sweatpants.*

Women are blessed with lots and lots of extra ways to win or lose validation. If you're a woman, you'll be judged on your beauty and your wit and how often you smile. You'll be judged on how much hair you have in some places and not in others. You'll be judged on whether you can get away with that outfit. You'll be judged on whether you're funny or just think you're funny. You'll be judged on the color of your wedding dress and whether you have an opinion that matters or a husband or children. Speaking of, you'll be judged on when you want children and how you have them. You'll be judged on who helps take care of your children in a way your husband or butch wife is not. Culturally, traditionally, historically, no matter how far we've come, most of us still put ourselves on pedestals to receive (or not receive) tiaras and wedding proposals.

Some books will tell you to accept yourself and all your flaws. To embrace your curves. You should probably do that if you can. That kind of ridiculous, enlightened talk never got me where I wanted to go unless where I wanted to go was my refrigerator to binge on Reddi-wip straight into my mouth and then to the couch to binge on Benedict Cumberbatch. (Curves are great on other people. Me—I'd like to look like a flapper with a touch of dysentery. Sorry for the digression; that's the stevia talking.) This is a book that tells you you're okay just the way you are if the way you are is someone with a palm that doesn't mind being smacked with a high five.

Still, it's fair to call myself a recovering junkie. I (finally) married a man who loves me the way I am. This is a dubious choice on his part, but I'm going with it. Not trying to get him to love me frees up a lot of hours in the day that I used to spend trying to dominate in yoga class after eating fat-free ice cream in my car during my first marriage. Also, I got older. Increasingly, people making decisions about my talent are my age or younger, and seeking approval from someone who can't sing *The Facts of Life* theme song is not a good use of my time.* And then, not easily, I became a mother. If you seek approval from someone who thinks it's hilarious to do downward dogs in his diaper while he farts, you are an approval masochist.

I don't think hitting rock bottom as an approval junkie means you stop questing for the big O[vation]. I was on my hands and knees, quite literally, when I hit rock bottom, the realization that I could never truly please my first husband (now wasband) having left me gulping for air, because I finally stopped gasping for love. Hitting rock bottom means you stop trying too hard, too often, and for the wrong person. There is a point when groveling for validation is dangerous. The extremes—such as questing for physical perfection

---

* As a tiny approval junkie, I was a tragically obedient child. So much so that when *The Facts of Life* premiered, and my parents told me I couldn't watch it, I didn't. Even though they were out of the house, enjoying their disco lesson. Somehow, though, soon after that, I did start watching *The Facts of Life.* Obviously there was nothing to worry about since it took me thirty-three years to realize that it was Cousin Geri who was the lesbian and not Jo.

or absorbing emotional abuse—can hurt you. Yet if you harness a fraction of that needy energy, you can prove something to yourself, rather than seeking the approval of others.

But if you've tasted any success, you still want to chase the dragon. I, for one, don't want to totally *re-cover*. Because I like staying somewhat exposed, a little raw. It means I stay open, to be wounded, yes, but also touched. It means I get to surprise myself by becoming more than I am. I'm wary of total self-acceptance. I'd rather fail dramatically than risk complacency.

Let's be honest, an approval junkie can get pretty tedious if she's constantly asking for appreciation but not dancing like a monkey to earn it. She'd be a busker with no instrument. You're not going to put money in her guitar case unless she's strumming something.

So here's my song. These are my stories. Maybe some of them will speak to you, even if you didn't welcome two different national news crews to follow you to your egg retrieval or crowdsource what to wear to your divorce. While I'm pretty sure you didn't ask your gay brother for a demonstration of how to give a killer hand job, I do feel certain that you, too, have occasionally yearned to be loved or applauded or laughed at in the very best way. And that you've striven to be more than you are before learning that approval of your own life is called gratitude.

I hope you enjoy this. Obviously.

No Bangs for the Bucks

"Why aren't you as pretty as I want you to be?"

I once paid someone $130 to ask me that.

She was this acting guru named Lesly Kahn, and my pilot season auditions were sucking, and I was told she was THE person to work with me. Now first let me explain what sucking means. Sucking is when you go to an audition, and the person going in before you is Mallory Keaton, née Justine Bateman, who has gone for a bold, unkempt Miss Havisham look with her eyebrows. I'm sorry if that sounds mean, because I totally wanted to look like her in the '80s, due to her unparalleled ability to rock narrow-wale cords.

Then you notice who's slated to go in right after you. Who? Oh, nobody but TRACI FUCKING LORDS, YES "FUCKING," BECAUSE SHE STARTED HER CAREER AS AN UNDERAGE PORN STAR. So you begin to realize that in the eyes of Hollywood or your agent or Dr. T. J. Eckleburg, that you, "the Faith Salie type," fall somewhere on the spectrum between a hirsute former sitcom star and a porn-celebrity-turned-method actor, which is to say that no one in show business knows what he wants, and you really, REALLY should have stayed in grad school one more year instead of hightailing it to LA before you got "too old" for sitcoms at age twenty-five.

And so you go in to read for a stony-faced casting director and a couple of producers, and you try very hard to convince them <u>you're</u> what they want: you're the funniest, prettiest, skinniest, hottest, archest, winsome-est, whatever-est. But *trying* is never a good thing in acting, and, when it comes to auditions, you are way better at trying than *being*. Then, as you are leaving the audition, you see Victoria Jackson, sporting short, stonewashed jean overalls, with her game face on for the same role, and you will truly turn anywhere for guidance.

Like to Lesly Kahn.

My manager at the time, having noticed I was getting cast less often than Justine Bateman shapes her brows, suggested a thirty-minute "private" with Lesly Kahn to help me get a job. Or at least a callback. For $130 a half hour (and a half hour was twenty-five minutes on the Kahn klock), I was hoping for more—like maybe oral sex or dark chocolate—but the least I expected was to walk out of our session feeling prepared for my next audition. Perhaps she charged that much in order to buy a vowel, because I have never seen "Lesly" spelled that way. At any rate, I drove from my apartment in Santa Monica to her school in Hollywood one night. The fact that her devotees call it "The Khanstitute" made me hope Ricardo Montalbán would be waiting for me, ready to run lines, all open shirted and silver foxy mulleted.

Lesly Kahn sat in the back of a serene candlelit room and exuded peacefulness. She barely spoke above a whisper.

A trim brunette, she fell somewhere in the late forties to early sixties age range—it's so hard to tell in the Land of Shiny and Smooth. She was surprisingly nurturing for the leader of the Khanstitute. I read my sides with her. ("Sides" are what they call your lines for an audition. I have no idea why but you feel cool when you first move to LA and get to flex this lexicon.) There was a long pause when I was done, and she was studying me so intently that I actually dared to hope she was about to say something like, "I don't know why you're not a massive star." Instead, she squinted her eyes, cocked her head sincerely, and, with compassionate bewilderment, uttered those words:

"Why aren't you as pretty as I want you to be?"

I've answered a lot of unusual questions in my life. Once I was asked in an interview, "If I told you there is a pink elephant in this room, how would you prove me wrong?" When I was twenty-six, and my mother was struggling through her final days with cancer, she asked me if I could let her go. And, on my first honeymoon, my wasband gazed at me over a romantic dinner in Barcelona and queried, "Did you ever break your nose?"

Lesly Kahn's was a shocking question, but by no means unanswerable. First of all, I agreed with her—I wasn't as pretty as *I* wanted me to be, and on top of that, I felt very bad that I was letting down Lesly Kahn, whose valuable time I was stealing from other actors with more facial symmetry.

"Your features are sharp; there's a softness missing."

This was true, both literally and metaphorically. I was desperately unhappy and unhappily desperate—disillusioned and competitive. Should I answer her by explaining that for me, at the time, life was a zero-sum game? That whenever someone got anything I wanted—a job, say, or a baby—I experienced it as a personal loss, as if the ledger of the cosmos were taunting me? Should I tell her I'd recently come really close to getting a part on the new TV show my wasband was producing? That he'd actually created a role for me—a character named *Hope,* no less ... and I didn't get it? That the head of the network didn't want me? Meaning I wasn't good enough to play myself. Or maybe I wasn't pretty enough to play myself.

Was it worth detailing how one actress who did land a role on my wasband's show was *someone I used to babysit*? And another was someone from the children's musical theater group I performed with back when I was a teenager and she was in her single digits? We three were not up for the same role, mind you—oh no, the seven years I had on them left me auditioning in the mother-to-middle-schoolers carpool lane while they were cast on the ingenue fast track. On the afternoon my wasband and I set aside to choose his wedding ring, he had to negotiate this girl's contract because *another* network also wanted her. Parked in front of the jewelry store, he paced outside the car on his cell phone, urgently but capably ensuring this little lady with whom I once danced jazz squares would star in his show. I sat inside the car, age thirty-four, appalled I'd allowed myself to get so old.

I didn't answer her question.

"Have you ever tried . . ."

What? What should I try, Lesly Kahn? Tell me and I'll do it. Cupping? Kombucha colonics? (Please not Scientology.) Fewer vowels in my name?

"Bangs?"

Boom. BANGS. My gigantic forehead might be all that was standing in the way of my dream. I'd been overthinking everything. Rehearsing my lines too much, unearthing subtext where there needn't be. This was a deeply superficial metanoia. I was relieved and so, so grateful—the simplicity of her prescription gave me hope. And then Lesly Kahn added something, as if it were an afterthought.

"Do you have children?"

No, I told her. I didn't go into the fact that my husband wasn't eager to have sex with me and that I never had any idea when I'd have my period and that my groovy lesbian gynecologist (from whom I hid when I saw her in the aisle of Ralph's supermarket, because it's just too awkward to see your OB-GYN when you are clothed from the waist down) had been telling me that I really needed to start trying to get pregnant if I ever wanted to have kids.

No kids, not yet, I told her. I want to.

"Because you should be a mother. You're supposed to have babies, I can tell. And then all this tension I see in you will disappear. I'll see you one day in the future and you'll be . . . you'll be happy . . . and the work will come because you'll have a different energy. You'll be . . . softer."

It was crazy, but I knew she was right. I left, feeling profoundly understood.

I called my wasband from the dark Hollywood parking lot in my leased 5-series BMW that I'd thought would make me feel like a baller, but in which I'd recently curled up fetally in the backseat, on the night I learned I couldn't even get cast as myself on my own husband's show, and sobbed like I hadn't since my mother died, years before.

"Something important just happened. I need to have . . . *bangs*."

A decade, a new career, a new city, and a new husband later, I had a baby.

And then another.

The bangs, on the other hand, turned out to be too much of a commitment.

Howler Monkey

I've only heard a howler monkey once.

I was in a remote jungle in Belize at 6:30 in the morning. I was filming a piece on ants. (Ants are pretty amazing, by the way. Do you know that Southwest Airlines used algorithms based on ant behavior to figure out the most efficient boarding process? I know it doesn't seem efficient when a couple of grandparents in baggy jorts are blocking the aisle with their sheer Middle American confusion, but it's not the ants' fault.) The only other people with me were the producer, who was also the cameraperson, our eager and compact Belizean guide, improbably named Vladimir, and our myrmecologist, a scientist who studies ants.

The myrmecologist looked remarkably like the Swedish Chef from the Muppets, and he had a substantial belly over which stretched an eye of the tiger T-shirt. Not a T-shirt celebrating the hit Survivor song, but a depiction of an actual menacing tiger and its eye, the likes of which I hadn't seen since perusing the design options for airbrush half-shirts in Daytona Beach circa '82.

We were doing a "walk and talk"—I was asking him ant-related questions on camera—when the entire canopy above us started to shake, and I heard a sound that stunned me. I grabbed Eye of the Tiger's arm. "Oh. My. God." I said. Like any teenager would, except I was a thirty-nine-year-old journalist on a news program. "Howler monkeys," he said.

It was a sound like I had never heard. And not at all what I expected a howler monkey to sound like.

I thought a howler monkey would sound shrill, strident, screechy. The reason I expected high-pitched clamor was because my wasband used to tell me, when I got upset, that I was a howler monkey. He also said I was a shrieking harpy. Not being overly familiar with the aggression calls of primates, I ignorantly assumed that a howler monkey's howls and a shrieking harpy's shrieks were homophonic: piercing and querulous—just what you'd want in a woman. When my howls and shrieks turned into sobs—when we'd fight about why he wanted a prenup or with whose family we'd spend the holidays—my wasband would tell me I was disturbing the neighbors, so I would go into my bathroom, turn on the shower, and sob there.

To be fair, he also called me lots of names that I loved. They made me giggle. They can be broken down into a few categories.

Sweet and Meaningful

"Blip" was the first nickname he called me. Sometimes it was "Blippy." The wasband didn't like to talk about his personal life, but when I came along, apparently he told his mother, "There's a blip on the radar."

He was pathologically private. One time, after we were married, he smelled especially good, so I asked if he was wearing cologne. He refused to tell me or let me continue to sniff him. He didn't want me to see him naked. He didn't want to share a mailing address or even a grocery shopping list—he would go to the market alone on a stealth food mission. He also didn't want me to show our wedding photos to anyone, including family or friends, who had flown to Scotland and donned kilts for our wedding. This was particularly sad for the sizable number of Jewish guests for whom it will presumably be a long time, like probably never, before they'll wear tartan skirts again.

But because my wasband was so private and had invited me in, I felt special. And because he was so handsome and confident and funny, he was very special. It was imperative, then, to stay special in his eyes, particularly as I'd volunteered to live in a world in which I kept asking to be chosen—to feel meaningful, I needed strangers to cast me. If those strangers weren't deeming me special, I desperately needed him to. And I longed to be more than a blip.

Little Names at Large

Like "Little," which he spelled "Lyiddlllelll" for no other reason than sheer silliness. He also called me "Little American," because it was so ridiculous and meaningless that it made us both laugh. As someone who has had body issues since I had to start wearing a bra at age nine, you can imagine how much I loved to be called little. I got my period at eleven. I "became a woman" in a Stuckey's restroom on a family drive to Disney World. They give out buttons at Disney World that say "1st Visit" and "Happy Birthday." What they do not offer—and clearly should—is a button that says "Happy Menarche!" Tweens experiencing their first menses can wear it at a character breakfast with spunky, bleeding Disney princesses. The second time I got my period was at an Air Supply concert a few months later. Perhaps God was punishing me for being at an Air Supply concert by telling me to wear white shorts that evening. I spent many years trying to use my gigantic spiral perm to distract from my ample curves and finally solved it all by becoming a borderline anorexic ninety-five pounds. After five glorious, chilly, amenorrheic years, people started to tell me I looked "healthy," which, if you have ever been happily, painfully skinny, feels as if someone is shaking your love handles while saying, "Way to go!!" So . . . I loved that my wasband was a six-two former Division I lacrosse player who always made me feel comparatively tiny, even if I constantly felt I had eleven pounds to lose.

But he wasn't just big in stature. He was big to me because he was, in my eyes, my future. We met when we were both twenty-four, the summer I moved from England to Los Angeles, introduced by a mutual friend in an encounter during which I found him arrogant and he found me snobbish. Like half of the beginning of *Pride and Prejudice*. I thought he was hot, so I maturely tried to make him jealous by mentioning the long-distance boyfriend I had at the time, and he returned the favor by hitting on my best friend. Again, all quite Austenian. I couldn't forget about him because our friend kept updating me on the wasband's health: not long after we met, he was diagnosed with cancer.

This friend also updated the wasband on me. He

informed him of my big breakout role as a guest star on *Star Trek: Deep Space Nine.* The wasband stayed home the night my episode aired, and—he later told me—as he watched, he asked God to bring me to him, which is possibly the nerdiest/most romantic thing ever.

By the time we remet three years later, he was quieter and leaner, hair just growing back from the chemotherapy. I, too, was humbled. Despite having recently been beamed up, my career was not stellar, but mostly I was bowed by grief. While he'd been beating cancer, cancer had beaten my mother.

I also learned his brother had died a few years earlier. We felt like we would find recovery in each other.

He wanted to feel big again, like he could take on the world after hanging on to his life, and I wanted to feel little enough to be held by him. There was a lot of sweetness to our early days. Enough that we spent a decade trying to recover it.

Little Butt Names

Like "Princess Little Butt." For some reason, my wasband thought my butt was hilariously small. It is NOT, by the way. My other nicknames in this category were "Plum Butt," "Mini Twin Turbos," and "Dual Blues." "Dual Blues" did not refer to my eyes, which are green, but to the fact that one day my wasband decided that my butt was so tiny, it looked like two blueberries. He then taped a picture of two blueberries to my bathroom mirror. This made me very happy; cf. egregious body issues above.

My wasband loved my body. He used to applaud if he

caught me in any state of undress. Even in his wedding toast, he made almost everyone but me feel uncomfortable by proclaiming, "Have you *seen* Faith naked?" (A few of our wedding guests had <u>not</u>, in fact.) This was amazing. This was confusing. He hardly wanted to ravage me. But I will always be grateful for the body confidence he gave me in a town where it's easy to forget what a real body looks like.

Bedtime Appearance

"Frankenstein's Pretty Little Baby" and "Sleepy Time Crash" fall into this category. This was because I prepared myself for sleep by putting in a retainer, an eye mask, and fluorescent pink-and-yellow-striped earplugs. Apparently I looked like Frankenstein's Pretty Little Baby, because I sported this klugey assortment of parts above the neck, and the neon earplugs sticking out of my earholes reminded him of the bolts sticking out of Frankenstein's neck. Also, the gear that protected me from sunlight, sound, and shifting teeth made me appear suited up for some kind of crash test. This ad hoc getup wasn't exactly attractive, so you're probably thinking, *Of course he didn't want to have sex with you when you looked like you were in some kind of hostage situation.* But this was after many sexless years of my trying, at bedtime, to look attractive or at least not like I had been kidnapped by terrorists who nevertheless wanted me to maintain orthodontic integrity.

So why did he almost never want to have sex with me? It wasn't total bed death, since he did occasionally perform CPR on me with his tongue—and a man that skillful at oral sex clearly wasn't gay. I figured it was my fault. I felt responsible, because sometimes at night, when I washed off my makeup, I'd lean into the mirror, far closer than anyone who loves herself should, and I'd pick at my face. This was something I'd long been doing—attempting to extract my imperfections. I was trying to make myself perfect when all I was really doing was vividly marking my own disapproval. Then my wasband would tell me I looked damaged and that made him feel sad for me rather than attracted to me. This did nothing except send me into a shame spiral that brought me closer to the mirror.

If I'd been gentler to myself, things might have been different. Or he could have been gentler to me—seeing me like that, he might have chosen to embrace me. But even on countless nights over the years when my face was unpillaged, and all I wanted was for him to pillage me consensually, we rarely connected in that way. I think our lack of sex life came down to power. The wasband was a man of power. He was powerfully built, powerfully persuasive, and he trafficked in power—he sold people's ideas and managed their careers, including, eventually, mine.

A person who wants to be in power gives when it suits him. The wasband shut down when he perceived I wanted something from him—such as an "I love you" or a proposal or sex. The more he sensed I longed for intimacy—not so much out of desire but out of desire to be wanted—the less we had. I guess he saw giving me what I wanted, when I wanted it, as a diminishment of his agency—an anathema to an agent. I could never initiate it, just receive it: every other month or so, he chose arbitrary times like when I was fast asleep or fully dressed and about to leave to suggest getting it on.

Sex became a reward for the rare span of days in which we'd not fought. Toward the end of our relationship, even as we talked (again) of separating, we took a long-planned trip to Peru. Perhaps because, by that time, we were being so open about our dismal future, our normally tense dynamic was deflated and easy. One night in Cusco, clearly intending to compliment me, he said, "If you acted like this all the time, I would want to have sex with you every day."

The kicker was, the sex was pretty good, occasionally superb. I wanted more all the time, because I wanted more of him in every way.

Froggy

Thanks in large part to my mad skillz with an eyelash curler and mascara, my wasband thought my eyes looked big enough to call me Froggy. He himself had beautiful eyes that fell somewhere between blue and gray.

But not long after that, "Froggy" took on a different cast as our marriage devolved. He was working all the time and I wasn't. Neither of us was supportive of the other. He named my requests for attention "needy." My then-therapist Fran told me I was just wanty. Then she explained to me that a frog placed in boiling water will hop out to save itself. But if you are a nascent serial killer, and you turn the water temperature up gradually, the frog will stay put until it finally dies in water that has reached boiling. She suggested I was the frog, and I'd gotten so used to my needs not being met that I was hardly noticing I had unfulfilled, legitimate needs. I never recognized cause for a dramatic escape jump, so I just sat there, slowly expiring.

If this was true—although it turns out the whole frog-in-boiling-water scenario has been scientifically disproven, but Fran's not a biologist, and that's not the point—if this metaphor was true, then I take ownership for being a pretty inert, dumb frog. Why did I stay so long when things were less than 50 percent good? For starters, the wasband and I were two people used to getting what we wanted. He not only topped my list of ambitions, he shared ambition with me and for me. It didn't matter how bad things got—he was my goal. I wanted to be the woman he thought I could be. He once told me that when we were apart, he'd think about all the things he loved about me and imagine how it would be to see me. And then when he would see me, I was never in reality as sweet as he'd imagined. But I wanted to be his dream girl—he kept trying to cast me in a role I was determined to play, so I kept auditioning. All this happened at that age—from your late twenties to midthirties—when you think thirty is a big deal, and thirty-five equals a spontaneous hysterectomy, when you have to attend a wedding every month, and you fear being left behind by life. I focused on my age and the age of everyone around me. I counted every day with him as an investment I didn't want to risk pulling out of.

The primary reason I was a hot froggy, though, was that I loved him. I loved him so much, to the exclusion of much else.

One day Fran told me to sit on the carpet of her office. It offered a nice thick pile, as it should have for the price of her fifty-minute sessions. I sat down dutifully, and Fran instructed me to draw a circle around myself. She said that circle was my state of mind. Then she asked me to draw a circle inside the big one that represented how much of my state of mind was taken up with thinking about him and feeling hurt, guilty, anxious, and neglected in my relationship. I drew a circle that took up about 80 percent of the bigger one. She then told me to sit inside the part of my rug-mind-circle that I dedicated to myself and my happiness, that is, inside the remaining 20 percent. Even Princess Little Butt couldn't fit in that space. I had made him—and him and me—virtually my whole life. I had left myself about one butt cheek's worth of self-possession.

Themeless Absurd

"Tits Malloy, Chi Town's Most Infamous Crimefighter." I don't have a lot of explication for this one, except I think it started because I was always cold (yes, even in LA—and not because I was too thin) and had the nipples to announce it. He used to call them "croissant nipples," something I will only share if you promise to believe me that my nipples aren't that big. Nor are they crescent shaped. Once you have breastfed, you realize what a big nipple truly looks like. Not only that, you also marvel that your nipples somehow turn into magic slinky straws, and you can basically lunge across the room to get something while your baby stays four feet behind, still sucking away. Your kid gets to keep one end of your nipple, and you get to take the rest of it with you.

We were sillier with each other than with anyone else in the world. Playfulness pervaded our dynamic. If we were walking down the street, he thought it was fun to nudge me gently with his broad shoulders and then order me to do the same to him, as hard as I could. Sometimes I think he wanted to roughhouse with me in the way that he would have with his late brother. Even when we were holding hands, he liked to do this thing where he'd squeeze mine and then I was supposed to squeeze back, with just a tiny bit less pressure. And then he would squeeze with even less pressure and so on, until one of us won by squeezing so imperceptibly that we'd argue if there had been a squeeze at all. Every gesture of physical affection was tinged with competition.

Other favorite games included Pillow Fort, which involved his surrounding me with walls of pillows on the bed so that I couldn't move. (This became less and less fun as our cohabitation progressed and he often took to constructing a high-thread-count bulwark in between us so there was no chance of our touching in our sleep.) Then there was Try to Get Away, in which he would pin me down or detain me in some way—never painfully—and I'd have to use all my strength to attempt to move myself. He found this endlessly delightful and so did I, until it got tedious. Releasing myself was out of the question—he was so much stronger than I was—but I was supposed at least to try. If I just gave up, if I didn't attempt the impossible, he was very disappointed and would declare, "You're no fun." Game over.

We were exhausting to be around. I was told this on separate occasions by his mother and my brother. The public giddiness of how we chummed along created an uneasy spectacle for those who knew and loved us best, because they understood the fragility of our bon temps. I only understand how enervating our company must have been now that I'm in a relationship that's literally unspectacular. Even when my now-husband John proposed to me, he didn't kneel. If you were watching us get engaged in Rome's Piazza

Navona, you were probably thinking, *That couple standing in front of the fountain sure likes to hug a lot.*

There's a fancy name for what your beloved calls you: *hypocorism.* "Sweetie," "Cupcake," "Junebug," "Eggroll" (which my friend Gideon calls his wife)—all those pet names are hypocoristic. And I don't think you need a masters in psychology to figure that the nicknames you and yours call each other say something—probably a lot—about your relationship.

My husband, John, calls me "baby." Even though that's a pretty ubiquitous hypocorism, it feels special to me, since no one else has ever called me that. I love it as long as I try not to remember how much Nick and Jessica used it on *Newlyweds.* And I will grant you that most hip-hop songs feature a gentleman protagonist calling a stranger "baby" in order to get in her pants, but my husband is a nice Jewish boy, and when he talks, he sounds like a sexier Alan Alda. So you can understand that his "baby" is earnest.

John calls me "baby" so often that I can't recall his ever calling me "Faith." Even if we're in public—say, in a store—and he needs to get my attention, he doesn't say my name; he does this cute little bird whistle to call me. He's made that whistle a million times, but it always transports me to Morocco. For our first New Year's, we were staying in Essaouira, on the Atlantic coast. And the open air lobby was a palm-and-orange-tree-filled atrium, at the top of which stretched a huge star made out of strings of lights—the pentagram of Morocco. I was eating a lazy and indulgent breakfast in the sun, under the star. And among the birds chirping, an incessant call started to emerge. It was probably going on for about a minute before I looked up and saw my patient (then) boyfriend staring down at me, from nine floors up, peacefully smiling. So whenever I hear John's inimitable bird call, even in the middle of Bloomingdale's Home Goods, it feels wistfully intimate.

"Baby" is also how he treats me: not in a diminishing way, but in a way that says you are mine; you are my responsibility; you have given me your heart, and I will take care of it, feed it, and keep it warm.

He is unconscious of all this, of course. But I'll take the constancy and lack of playfulness in this hypocorism over the exhausting psychic noogies of my old nicknames any day. Someone who calls you "baby" invites you to cry in his arms, not in the shower.

During my divorce process with the wasband, he had to send me some mail. It was always addressed to "faith salie" in a smaller font than the address, with no caps, like I was e. e. cummings's redheaded stepchild. And the return address had his name in all caps, sort of like this: "WAS BAND." It reminded me of the screen saver he'd always had, for at least the decade I knew him, on each of his computers. Floating by, on a loop, were these words in big caps: "I WILL ALWAYS WIN."

He didn't win when he married me. I didn't make him happy, and I couldn't make myself happy. My heart shrunk for a while there. I got little in the worst way.

I'm a writer; I want to construct a narrative that explains why we fell apart. But I can't, not neatly at least. I rather envy those people who have an uncomplicated breakup story—you catch your husband doing coke in a sex swing you never installed or his other wife calls to find out where he is. Or someone says, "I just don't love you anymore."

That's like a sharp knife cleanly cutting the relationship apart. My marriage was sawed gradually by a dull, serrated knife. And only in retrospect, with retelling, does the severance become sharper, not duller, because I can understand it better.

They say (and sing) the first cut is the deepest. I don't think so. The cut that's the deepest is the one with the guy you were crazy about. I'm not crazy about John. I'm sane about John. I've got scar tissue, and I'm not worried about his cutting me. I was crazy about my wasband. I pinned all my happiness on him. I made him my human Pinterest board.

Maybe it's enough to tell you that near the end of our relationship he was calling me "Salie," and at the very end, before we stopped speaking altogether, I was "Faith."

And that howler monkey in Belize—the thing my wasband told me I sounded like? Its sound . . . it was the opposite of a petulant shriek. Its roar was huge, terrifying, guttural, deep, primal. It was fierce. It shook the jungle. It didn't carp; it proclaimed itself.

The howler monkey's howl tells me one of these two things: either my wasband was wrong all along, and he didn't know what a howler monkey really sounded like . . . or I'd been underestimating myself. I had no idea how powerful I really was.

Miss Aphrodite

When I graduated from North Springs High School in Atlanta, Georgia, home of the Spartans, the most famous alumnus was one John Schneider, a.k.a. Bo Duke from *The Dukes of Hazzard*. More recent notable grads are Usher and Raven-Symoné, and you can decide for yourself who's more famous based on your appreciation of R&B versus a bizarrely silent accent aigu. Of course, I myself am famous among certain circles, if you can make a circle out of three people. Those three would be my dad, my dad's accountant, who kindly asks for updates on my career, and the one *Star Trek* überfan who possesses the collectible trading card featuring me as genetically enhanced mutant Serena Douglas.

I can say this about all those NSHS celebrities who are way starrier than I: none of them was crowned Miss Aphrodite.

Now that my old high school is a charter school, and we are in the twenty-first century, I'm pretty sure they've shut down the beauty and talent pageant that marked the highlight of my time as a Spartan. If you're shocked that a public high school held a pageant for its girls every spring, then your people were probably on the chilly side in the War of Northern Aggression.

Winning the pageant became a goal of mine early on during freshman year. My personal mandate to make straight As included an A for Aphrodite. Throughout high school, I was in classes with mostly the same people all day long. Shira Levine, Alfred Chang, Greg Kaplan—you get the picture: we were the honors students. As soon as the bell rang at the end of the day, I rushed away from school to activities that required character shoes and emphatically splayed fingers that a Philistine might deride as "jazz hands." I was building a serious professional career in touring kids' musicals, Six Flags over Georgia commercials, and public service announcements about recycling and just saying no. In other words, I didn't get to participate much in Spartan extracurriculars. Lots of the other girls, with names like Kelli Crump and Romney Ramsey, were cheerleaders or on drill team, and they bonded at practice on the football field, which was officially called Thermopylae Stadium. (North Springs did not have a classics department, which might explain why our stadium was named after a battle in which the Spartans fought valiantly but were ultimately routed. Our school paper was *The Oracle*, the yearbook was *The Phalanx*, and my permed hair was Medusa.) Do most high schools have drill teams? I'm not sure, so in case you've never heard of one, just picture a bunch of cute long-haired girls in a flash mob with glow sticks and white go-go boots. The drill team danced to Devo's "Whip It" and *Ferris Bueller's* "Oh Yeah" while I was in downtown Atlanta singing *Starlight Express* tunes and neutered versions of Sondheim. I felt like no one at NSHS understood what I could <u>really</u> do—which was belt loudly and overemote. I needed to show them. I needed to be Miss Aphrodite.

I knew just enough Greek mythology to know that Aphrodite was the goddess of beauty and love. Love, I wasn't after. I had love—a family who loved me, a couple of boyfriends who'd loved me and gone on to college. As a freshperson, sophomore, and junior, I went on dates and to a couple of proms. By senior year, love could wait, because having a boyfriend seemed like a distraction from the goal at hand, which was beauty.

What high school girl doesn't think about beauty? Girls are always volunteering for beauty jury duty, judging themselves and others. This pageant meant I was volunteering to be judged publicly. Unfortunately, like most teenage girls, I always thought I'd look better if I were thinner. But I didn't obsess over it, because I was too busy figuring out whether cobalt blue eyeliner applied to the inner rim made my eyes look bigger or smaller and how tall I could build my hair. Until senior year.

By my last year of high school, I had a new definition of beauty. For me, it was losing so much weight that people pointed and stared, that I could wear anything, that I was a fat-free product. Loveliness was being so skinny that I looked like a real dancer, a triple threat, even though my threat level was barely two and a half. It was the makeover I'd given myself. Probably anyone looking at me didn't see beauty as much as bones, but I finally liked what I saw in the mirror—or, rather, what I didn't see, all that flesh that I'd disappeared. I remember learning as a teenager that Michelangelo saw his statues inside marble and carved until he set them free. Just shy of my eighteenth birthday, I felt triumphant that I'd finally chiseled myself into an angular work of art. I wanted to put the art on display in the gym. But it took me four years until I got sculpted. And it took me four years to get that tiara.

There was an unwritten rule that only a senior could snare the title. I knew I could compete as a freshman, but I understood I had to pay my dues. You had to get a club to sponsor you, so I always represented French Club. This wasn't difficult since no one else in *le* club wanted to compete. But I preferred to think French Club recognized my *je ne sais quoi*, which I was about to unleash in the school gymnasium.

Every Miss Aphro (as we called it) opened with a group dance number. It was usually some kind of '60s ditty like "Do You Love Me?" to which we could all bop around. We were divided into three groups, according to our <u>perceived</u> dance talent. I was perceived to be of middling dance talent, which I felt put me at a distinct disadvantage. We were supposed to believe that it was all good fun and we weren't being judged, but who's *that* stupid? I wasn't, which is why I rolled my eyes when I was always assigned to the literal group: I was one of the girls who had to stand there twisting and mashing invisible potatoes while the hipless girls got to jeté and tumble. Despite my remedial dance placement, I was very satisfied to place first runner-up in my first pageant. I chalk up my near win to two things: (1) my cobalt blue unitard and (2) my pandering answer during the interview portion.

It's hard to compete with cobalt spandex, but it's easy to compete <u>in</u> it, my friends. Especially when you add bright red dance panties over it that keep giving you a wedgie while you earnestly sing "Nothing" from *A Chorus Line*. "Nothing" is a song for a Latina character named Morales, and I am the whitest person on earth, but I sang the shit out of that song. Which was easy to do, since if you've ever heard the song, it's mostly kind of spoken. I let my shiny unitard do the real singing.

The judges would pick five of us for the interview round. You could qualify to judge Miss Aphrodite if you did something like run a real estate company or predict the weather on a local station or hold the title of Mrs. Peachtree City 1983. Freshman year, I'd already decided that no matter what my interview question was, I would answer, "Dr. Martin Luther King Jr." That seemed to be clutch, especially in Atlanta in the '80s when the city's slogan was the catchy "Atlanta: The City Too Busy to Hate." It just so happened that my answer lined up stunningly with my question, which was, "What person do you admire most and why?" Of course I did genuinely admire what I knew of MLK, but at that point in my life, the most truthful answer would probably have been "Molly Ringwald, because she is so awesome and then some."

You may be wondering about the talent offerings of my rivals. The competition was stiff. Stiff as in awkward and self-conscious. Just as Sparta was a city-state known for its military, not its arts, North Springs circa 1986–89 was not a high school known for its performers. There was no drama club, no spring musical. While Susan Woodworth always twirled a nonflaming baton, most of the young ladies vying for Miss Aphro chose to dance or sing. Song choices ranged

from the best of Sheena Easton (sadly, <u>not</u> "Sugar Walls")
to Whitney Houston (interminable renditions of "The
Greatest Love of All" with at least five key changes). Bitsy
Rieland played it safe, lip-synching "How Lovely to Be a
Woman" from *Bye Bye Birdie*. To stand out, you really had to
be creative in your mediocrity. So Wendy Taratoot sang all
of "The Rose" with one arm mysteriously behind her back
until the very last note when she whipped out her hand to
reveal that the whole time she'd been holding . . . *a rose!* Me-
lissa Terrell sang "Your Cheatin' Heart" and dedicated it to
her father, a man who loved his wife faithfully but who also
loved Hank Williams. Laura Djie came onstage dressed in
jodhpurs, rolling a TV and VHS player behind her. For her
talent, she hit play and treated the audience to a video of her
riding her horse—and possibly breaking her hymen—to the
"Love Theme from St. Elmo's Fire."

The one to beat was Stacy Walker. But I didn't want to
beat her, because she was one of my very best friends. Plus
she was a grade above me, so I magnanimously wanted her
to wait to win until I was a junior so she could then crown
me when I was a senior. Stacy was—and is—one of the
world's best dancers. She ended up touring around the world
with Michael Jackson and becoming one of his choreogra-
phers. Stacy could kick her leg up so high that her heel went
behind her head, but she only used this power onstage, not
in backseats with boys.

Sophomore year was a wash. I didn't even get to the
interview round. I sang a plaintive song about wanting to
be a lion tamer in a salmon-colored leotardy dress with
rhinestones all over it. Here's a pageant tip: never choose

your song from a forgettable 1970s Broadway musical that starred Doug Henning. I was so disturbed at the judges' blindness to my sparkly talent that I went home right after the pageant and ate a whole Domino's pizza with my boyfriend Brenden.

Not only did I get my groove back by junior year, but I got back, too. I was big. Big boobs, big butt, big hair. I was sixteen and had given up soccer and taken up cheese fries, now that I had my license and could drive to the mall. I'd eaten a lot more pizzas since the last pageant. But I had a kind of Delta Burke thing going on—I worked it in a navy blue dress that was half sequins and the other half tiers of chiffon. I upped my game and sang a Liza Minnelli song called "City Lights"—I didn't just sing it; I <u>sold</u> it in the direction of the local meteorologist as if to declare, "That's Liza with a 'Z,' fucker!!" I sailed through the interview round without even relying on slain African American icons and tied for first runner-up with Stacy Walker's younger sister Tiffany. Tiffany danced, too, and was somehow even skinnier and more flexible than Stacy. Tiff's secret weapon was to down a whole package of Fun Dip—which is basically Pixie Sticks in a pouch—right before going onstage. Obviously there was some crazy-awesome dance DNA in the Walker blood even though Tiffany was adopted from Korea. Stacy was finally a senior and therefore rightfully crowned Miss Aphrodite after her elastic hamstrings brought The Bangles' "Hazy Shade of Winter" to life.

By senior year, the stakes were at least as high as my hair. And my hair was so lofty that it refused to be confined by the borders of my senior photo and was therefore cut off at the top. This was my final chance for what I saw as closure on my high school career. The cherry on top of a crown on top of my curls.

I was ready to leave North Springs, but not without leaving my mark. On a date, I wouldn't go farther than second base, but I was on a macro trajectory out of that school, that town, that South. I didn't understand why all the kids around me wanted to stay close to home. Saving money on tuition by going to a state school is one thing, but driving a brand-new Iroc Z with UGA decals was another. I fantasized about lacing up L.L.Bean duck boots to trudge through stuff called "snow" as I walked across some two-hundred-year-old courtyard to a class called "Gender, Empire, and the Politics of Appearance." I was headed (in my mind) to study theater at an Ivy League School. And while I was so eager to leave it all behind, I also wanted to wear a sash and tiara for the departure on my Grand Tour. I've never been too cool for school.

So I was hungry for that title. I was hungry for everything—being named valedictorian, acceptance to Yale, and food. Since the fall of senior year, I'd lost forty-five pounds. I'd spent the summer at a precollege musical theater program staring loathingly at myself in dance classes taught by the likes of Billy Porter, who would go on to win a Tony for *Kinky Boots*. I returned home as resolute as Rocky, except with a high-cut leotard for aerobics instead of a hoodie for stadium stair-climbing. I lived on raw fruit and vegetables and a Blow Pop I allowed myself to suck and chew while I completed all my AP homework for five hours every night. I honored the Sabbath by consuming two fruit-flavored Mentos every Sunday morning. And although my daughter and nieces will read this someday, and I really ought to present

myself as a dangerous cautionary tale from an after-school
special, I must confess that I already felt like a winner even
before I vied for the title that final time.

There was always an entrance walk for each of the
contenders—you'd do your frozen smile strut toward the
judges down a rickety catwalk that stretched from the stage
into the basketball court. And during that walk, the emcee
would introduce you to the audience. That year, my introduction should have been, "Our next contestant is five foot
five and ninety-five pounds. Faith's hobbies include burning
more calories than she consumes, trying to stay warm, and
suppressing her menstrual cycle."

I was thin it to win it. Which is why I turned to Valerie
Kennedy.

Vocal coach Valerie Kennedy was the Béla Károlyi for
pageant hopefuls. She could take your voice, assign you
the perfect song and a few key moves, and turn you into
Miss Anything. She was the wee-est woman in the twee-
est home. She lived in a dollhouse painted Wedgewood blue
and white. Inside was all porcelain figurines and toile. And
a gleaming white piano where the magic happened. Valerie
used long spoons she collected from Dairy Queen Blizzards
as her secret weapon. When you'd sing, she'd make you stick
the spoon into your throat to maintain ideal palate placement. Luckily, I was anorexic and not bulimic, so this exercise proved very helpful. But even more helpful was Valerie's
keen choice of song for me—Barbra Streisand's "Let's Hear
It for Me" from *Funny Lady*. With lyrics that, at one point in
the song, actually request a standing ovation, Valerie and I
weren't playin':

I'm the number one attraction to see . . .
Come on kids, let's hear it for me!

To ensure I stuck the landing, Valerie taught me her signature Pageant Arm Raise. Please imagine this, and while
you imagine it, visualize me with my crunchy curls piled atop
my head, black patent pumps on my feet, and my bony body
sporting a rainbow-sequined micromini I'd bought from the
Avon catalog: I'm onstage, and for the very last note of the
song, I turn to my right. The microphone is in my left hand—
the one closest to the audience, the *downstage* hand, as theater geeks know. My right arm (*upstage!*) waits, straight
down at my side, poised for action. As I wail the last word of
the song—the "MEEEEEEEEEEEEEEEEEEEEEE!"—I
crouch delicately on my stilettos and rise up slowly while
simultaneously raising my outstretched right arm from six
o'clock to effing high noon. And I follow the arc of that glorious Pageant Arm with my entire head, so that as my jazz
hand is raised sky high, I am looking up to the Lord. And
at the end of it all, after I have held that note till queendom
come, I yank that arm down dramatically, demonstrating
that I have exhausted myself, that I have given you all of me
right there on that gym stage, leaving you no choice, kids,
but to hear it for me.

I hope I don't have to tell you it worked. Not to brag or
anything, but no one stood a chance against my emaciated,
spastic resolve. First runner-up was Tiffany Walker, who'd
broken her toe in rehearsals, presumably due to a Fun Dip
overdose. But like '96 Olympic gymnast Kerri Strug, who
taped her shredded ankle to bring home the gold, Tiff taped

her toe and landed victory adjacent. The outgoing goddess, the indomitable Stacy, visiting from Florida State University, managed to wedge that tiara into my Aqua Net nest.

High school obsessions seem so important at the time, the yearbooks full of senior superlatives—Best Legs, Best Smile, Best Dressed. I still have my tiara. It's missing a comb to shove it into my hair, and some stones have disappeared. Yes, I'm like a character in a Tennessee Williams play, clinging to a symbol of my salad days—like literally just salad, y'all, with dressing on the side.

About a week after I won, I received rejection letters from all the Ivys, and Jennifer Linde got to be valedictorian. On prom night, my dad took me out to dinner because no one had asked me. But for one brief shining moment, the Greek gods had smiled on me and welcomed me into their pantheon as Miss Aphrodite, Goddess of Beauty and Love.

I love casually telling people I won my high school pageant. In the Northeast, in this century, it sounds positively exotic. I faux-brag about being Miss Aphrodite 1989 because it's so ridiculous, but the truth is, I have a wistfulness about it. I remember it clearly as one of the last times I set goals—to dominate my body and to captivate the student body—certain I could achieve them through sheer determination. That's a faith that belongs to the young, because you learn soon enough that life doesn't work that way, and wishing hard and working hard don't always stick a crown atop your ephemerally skinny body.

Extra Vanilla

My mother liked to bake for criminals. She'd be driving us to or from Woodland Elementary School or soccer practice or dance class and spot a work gang of prisoners doing some kind of road repair. Mom would zip home and whip up some pumpkin and cranberry walnut breads. Then she'd pull her copper Datsun 280ZX over to the side of the road and drop the loaves off with the corrections officer in charge of the gang. The prisoners, possessing appreciative but not overly discriminating taste buds, called her "The Gingerbread Lady."

It was a fitting moniker, since my mom was famous for her gingerbread houses. For a couple of days, right at the beginning of Advent (that's the four weeks before Christmas for those of you without mothers who went to church every single day except Sunday, because going to Saturday vigil earns you one day off), Mom turned our kitchen into a delicious-smelling construction site. She baked turnkey homes, carefully covering the cooled burnt sugar soldering with royal icing piping. Sometimes she'd screw up and we'd hear profanities such as "Sugarfoot!" coming from the kitchen. She'd save one gingerbread house for my brothers and me to decorate and distribute the rest. My senior year of high school, she made and garnished five extra for all the teachers who'd written me college recommendations. She always dropped some off for her brothers' families. I liked going on that delivery run with her—she'd ask me to sing her Christmas carols while we drove to Uncle Dick's, Uncle Bob's, and Uncle David's. Mom would hop out of the car and quickly leave the naked houses in their garages along with all the gumdrops and nonpareils my cousins might need to adorn them. She didn't want to make a fuss, so we'd pull out of the driveway before she'd get discovered.

That was very my mom: wanting to spread deliciousness but not wanting attention for it. I may have inherited more of the first part.

Usually her goodies weren't on the fancy side, but birthday cakes called for preproduction meetings. Just as I would start discussing my visions in August for the Halloween costumes she'd sew me, we'd begin planning my cake around February for my April party. She took a decorating class and would practice making rosettes on wax paper at the kitchen table. As with any activity that required concentration, Mom stuck her tongue across her mouth so that the right side of her cheek stuck out for the duration of rosette crafting. (She also did the tongue-in-cheek thing when folding fitted sheets.) For most of my girlhood, she created some kind of doll cake where the cake was a massive skirt out of which rose a blond Barbie torso. I still dream of the fluffiest pale pink cake she decorated with glittery flowers made from marshmallows. Much later on, she figured out how to make me a completely fat-free Baked Alaska with angel food, frozen yogurt, and flaming meringue. (I have just now decided "Flaming Meringue" will be my name when I am reincarnated as a drag queen.)

This is why I can't buy a cake for my kids' birthdays. My husband offers to "keep it simple" for me by picking up something at this famous bakery on Madison. The thought that he occasionally had to buy his own birthday cakes in that very store when he was younger makes me so sad that I forbid it. He also works down the street from the Cake Boss and could easily bring home a two-foot blue macaw cake my son has requested that would be two hundred times better than anything I could create, but I can't do it. This kind of time-sucking sleeve rolling is part of what being a mother means to me.

You may not really consider how much you're like your mom if she's still around. Before you enter middle age, you may be too busy building your own life to catch a glimpse of yourself in the mirror and notice how, at a certain angle or when you are really tired, you look like her. It may surprise you one day to see yourself with her smile in a photo or hear yourself call your child "Pumpkin," just like your mom called you.

I surprised myself by putting on an apron.

Baking was a way to be close to my mom when I was little. I didn't really bake, though; I just stood beside her like an entropic sous chef. She invited me to measure and pour (implicit fractions lesson) and crack eggs. My master creation was a scrumptious treat called "Daddy's pie crust cookies" which, as you may gather, were "cookies" made from unused crust. Mom would give me scraps and encourage me to roll them in cinnamon sugar. We'd pop them in the oven, and I'd proudly foist them on my father when he got home from work. He appeared to love them—he always had a bite right away! It wasn't until years later that I learned he'd spit them into a napkin. I can't decide if my mom was focused on burnishing my culinary self-esteem or playfully torturing her husband. That's number 492 on the list of questions I'd ask her if I could. After, "What time exactly was I born so I can finally get a meaningful astrology chart?" and before, "Seriously, how is it possible you never used tampons??"

My mom was the den mother for my brothers' Cub Scout group. She found time for this, along with teaching Sunday school and making those terrifying dolls with shriveled apple heads, which is what twentysomething gals apparently liked to do in the '70s. One day when I was home with her as usual while my big brothers were at school, she was frosting a cake she'd decorated with some Scout emblem and realized she hadn't made enough icing. This posed a dramatic problem, since she was on a deadline and didn't have enough time to steer her gigantic station wagon to the A&P to get ingredients. I climbed up on my kitchen helper stool and, for the solid two minutes she spent fretfully plundering our cabinets in search of confectioners' sugar, I silently scraped up every last lick of icing I could find anywhere—on the side of the bowl, on the knife, on the spatula. I willed it to amass, like I was Jesus with the loaves and frosting. It made a nice lump. "Is this enough?" I asked her. Her eyes lit up, and she kissed me. We both watched, holding our breath, as she spread the icing to just barely, totally cover the cake. She must have told me and everyone how I'd "saved the day" for a week. My mother doled out generous servings of compliments.

By the time I got to college, the only thing I was interested in whipping up was a fresh dollop of feminism. A room of one's own was decidedly not the kitchen. Baking seemed retrograde, but what was worse to me at the time was that it involved fattening ingredients.

Then Mom died. There were more pernicious things in this world than butter and egg yolks. Like cancer.

Being the only daughter in our family, I inherited most of my mother's "stuff," for lack of a better word. I spent one of the bleakest afternoons of my life sitting on the floor of Mom's walk-in closet as I went through her clothes, inhaling her scent in hopes of being able to summon it on future command.

Her death was no surprise—thank you, cancer, for the heads-up—but my father still couldn't deal. He imposed a hasty deadline to sell the Florida house into which my parents had recently moved. My assignment was to save anything I might want and quickly send it to myself in LA. My sister-in-law gently helped me as much as she could, but how do you decide what to keep of your dead mother? I scavenged Mom's pockets as if I might find something worth saving when the only thing worth anything was gone. In her Christmas cardigan—because, yes, she was a mom who wore a sweater with gingerbread people appliqués—I found a shopping list. "Fiber One, bell peppers, 2%, berries, Metamucil." I pictured her popping into Kroger on her way home from 7:15 a.m. Mass.

I donated her clothes and saved her jewelry.

Then there were her recipes.

Mom wasn't a collector (nor am I, a trait manqué that has served me well in my itinerant life), but she left behind a trove of recipes. Recipes she jotted down on index cards. Recipes on cards with, "From the kitchen of [fill in name of one of her tennis partners here]" printed on top. In her careful handwriting, she'd given all the recipes a grade. (Question number 499: "Why keep a recipe graded B?") She'd made notes on the cards—things she changed or added. She always doubled, sometimes tripled, the vanilla extract.

Returning to Los Angeles after she was gone, three thousand miles away from everyone who loved me most, left me in a dark, hungry place. I tiptoed into my tiny kitchen and pored over the recipes as if they were scrapbooks of my childhood. Her handwritten lists of ingredients filled a bit of the void now that I was no longer receiving her weekly greeting cards filled with chatty updates and twenty-dollar bills for a manicure. Baking <u>was</u> retrograde, in the most therapeutic sense: once again, it was a way to be close to her. I pulled out the serious KitchenAid stand mixer she'd bought me and stocked up on vanilla.

I learned I love baking. And I learned why my mother loved it. Most people smile when you present them with something homemade. I love fulfilling requests—pumpkin bread for Kerrie, almond cream cheese bars for Mario, Kahlúa brownies for Uncle Juan. I'm no pâtissière; but I guess homemade treats are so rare in this busy day that the full-tummy, fulsome thanks I get seem disproportionate to my efforts. I have witnessed disciplined, chiseled homosexuals erupt into a gluten-free-for-all after a taste of my Fuzzy Navel cake with Peach Schnapps glaze.

I once gave someone a cake on TV. I appeared as a guest on *The Late Late Show*, and I was very very nervous, largely because I knew no one in the audience had any idea who I was. So I felt that delivering my Coca-Cola cake on air to then-host Craig Kilborn would be a cute icebreaker.

"I brought you a white trash cake!" I declared, thrusting it at him.

He was completely nonplussed. "You made this?" he said, not like, "Wow, you actually made this?!" but like, "That's really weird." Because it was.

"It's a Bundt!" I cried, desperately willing it to be a catchy punch line.

He put it on his desk, and I'm sure one of the camera guys took it home.

I food-pushed successfully, however, in the hospital after I'd given birth to my daughter. Just as I'd done for my son's birth, I'd arrived at the hospital towing a bag laden with tons of homemade desserts to give to the nurses during my stay. (Technically, I didn't arrive with that bag. I arrived with my eyes closed, leaking amniotic fluid and vomiting. My husband actually arrived with the bag, since I was busy wanting to die.) I wanted to thank those strangers who enter the most important, dramatic days of your life. These are ladies who check stitches you can't even see, change bloody sheets, and genuinely care that you produce a soft stool, ladies whom you'll never see again. The day we had to leave the hospital, one of the administrators came into my room and said he wanted to talk to my husband. Crazy with exhaustion, I decided that meant I was in trouble for waving away the one nurse who kept barging in to take my blood pressure just at the moment I'd been able to shut my eyes because my daughter had taken a short break from sucking the life out of me. Turned out, I wasn't in trouble. The staff was so appreciative of my baking that they wanted to thank us by giving us one free night, like a special offer at Hampton Inn.

Sometimes when I shuffle into work balancing Tupperware full of white chocolate Congo bars, I like to think I'm like my mother. I don't think my mom sought anyone's approval but God's. She didn't crave attention or a number on a scale. Her goals were modestly specific—volunteer to teach ESL, get her master's degree in comparative religion, don't eat a single peanut M&M until her son returned safely from a sojourn in immediate post-Soviet Russia. She simply lived to make other people happy, and by doing so, made herself happy. That was enough for her—more than enough, as she repeatedly marveled at how "blessed" she was.

"Vanilla" generally describes something or someone as ordinary or conventional. But if you think about it, vanilla is anything but. Vanilla is spicy—it's literally a spice. (The world's second-most expensive one after saffron—fun trivia fact for your next drunken cookie swap.) It comes from something as exquisite as an orchid. *The Book of Spices* characterizes vanilla as "pure and delicate." Too classy to beg for attention, it supports other ingredients. Vanilla doesn't need to be the star, but it enhances everything.

My mom was vanilla, extra vanilla at that. She brought warmth to any situation. She was supportive to the point of being deflective, always focused on encouraging others. And she was spicy. Yes, she read a Bible chapter a day, usually from the miniature Good Book she pulled out of the console in the 280ZX during long stoplights. But she also kept *Penthouse* in her bedside table. (I thought I was the only child who knew this until my brothers and I compared notes a couple decades later.) Once, when I was in college, we had a phone call that went like this:

ME: Hi, Mom, whatcha doing?

MOM: Hi, my darlin'! I just put in some Ben Wa balls and I'm making dinner.

ME: I'm sorry, what did you say?

MOM: I'm making din—

ME: No, before that. What balls where?

MOM: Oh, the Ben Was are these balls I put in my vagina to strengthen my pelvic floor. They're supposed to make sex even better! I just walk around with them in me. It's quite a workout.

Such was the flavor of my mother.

And just as vanilla gently infuses the whole dish, Mom was the sine qua non of our family. She still is ... her redolence fills the family we have become without her.

I don't bake so much anymore. I don't have the time. There's not enough room on our kitchen counter to leave out a mixer, and the thought of squatting and lifting the thing, then cleaning and putting it away again after lifting and cleaning and putting away children all day exhausts me. It would make too much noise to bake when kids are supposed to be sleeping. I also don't know how to cook for my family, so I feel vaguely guilty that the only things I ever make for them are on the apex of the food pyramid. But mostly I don't bake a lot because I don't feel compelled to. What started as a way to connect with my mother grew into a way to feel like I had something to offer. My life is fuller now. When it wasn't so full, I was trying to fatten everyone else up. These days, I bake because it's an occasion, or I really want to thank someone, or I have bananas that are so close to expiry that they're screaming to be transubstantiated into banana bread. I bake because it's meditative. I like the whir of the mixer, the taste of the batter, the smell of my efforts.

Since he's become a father, my brother David's really been the one to take up our mother's baking mantle/apron. He concocts ridiculous Dora the Explorer and My Little Pony cakes for his kids that involve sketches and all-nighters and way more counter space than I can ever hope to have in a Manhattan kitchen. We often call each other when we're baking to share Mom memories—momeries, if you will. When I texted him the photos of my Curious George monkey face cakes I made for Augustus—I made one vanilla, one Coke, as well as a practice one so that I didn't fail my two-year-old—David wrote back, "Wow—great job! Did you stick your tongue into the side of your cheek as you were 'piping'?"

I'll never bake and decorate as well as my mother, but I sometimes feel her energy in me when I'm bustling in the kitchen and handing off plates of Christmas wreath cookies to the doormen. It's like what my dad said in his eulogy for Mom: "We can't be as good as Gail. But we can all try to be good like her."

l Sing the Body Dysmorphic

l have virtually no regrets in my life. I couldn't have said this in my thirties. I can say it now, though, because I've experienced all these happy endings that are really beginnings. I've lost and gained husbands, jobs, babies, expensive sunglasses, weight, eyelashes, and it's all turned out (more than) okay.

But I do have one specific regret. I didn't go with my mom to the Basilica di San Marco for Mass on the only Sunday morning we would ever share in Venice. I didn't go because it was raining that morning, and I couldn't go for a run outside. So I stayed in our small hotel room, because I wanted to work out in it, alone. I didn't know then that it was the last trip my mother and I would ever take. What I did know was that I just *had* to work out.

Mom didn't mind. I didn't mind either, until years later, after she was gone. I returned to San Marco and wished I'd held her hand there during the Lord's Prayer in Italian, under its golden domes, instead of getting my forty-five minutes of cardio.

It seems that every memoiry, essayish book from a woman today includes at least a chapter about the author's body. This chapter usually contains ample self-deprecation (without which no woman can publish stories about herself), possibly a Spanx reference, and probably an apologetic anecdote about the one time she got relatively skinny. Descriptions of being chilly and cranky flesh out the tale. The reader may be served an intimate glimpse of the author's food diary. It concludes with some wearily empowering denouement about self-acceptance at any size. Everyone feels good about that kind of chapter.

This is not that kind of chapter. Because that is not my story.

If you've never stood backward on a scale and implored a nurse not to tell you what it says; if you've never considered rice cakes a sensible dinner or gone five years without getting your period and relished every minute of it; if you've never woken up at 4 a.m. so you could work out in the dark in a cabin in the Central American rain forest that has no power but has 90 percent humidity; if you've never cried alone in front of a dance studio mirror doing some kind of nonsurgical liposuction by pulling your thighs back with your hands; if you've never traveled around Europe as a student on Eurail lugging a scale wrapped in your college sweatshirt, then you may not understand this, or it may be boring or even offensive. If that's the case, I apologize. But there's absolutely no way to share honestly my quest for approbation without some of the details of my tortured crusade to be thin. It's a First World Upper-Middle-Class White Girl preoccupation to be sure, but I've not been enlightened enough to accept that who I am is way more than how much I weigh.*

So what shape does my chapter take? Should it be bloated with tales of control and despair, from how I ran laps around a Zimbabwe airport after an overnight flight to how I'd spend nights driving around Los Angeles the year after my mother died, buying cakes and muffins to eat in my car? Do I describe how I've been asked at the gym, more than once, whether I'm a stuntwoman** and, after my initial flush of pleasure, I wonder what that person is implicitly saying about my face? Or should this be a lean, bare-bones story that simply confesses that, although I weigh significantly more than I did at my nadir/zenith, I'm not at peace with my body, even if I'm grateful for it? The only advice I have to offer is eat just the crusts of breadlike fare, take the stairs, and try not to hate yourself too much.

The main trouble with this chapter—which really could be a book, but I have no stomach for the topic at that length, so ubiquitous has it been in my life—is that it has a beginning but no end. It opens in the halls of Woodland Elementary when a second-grade boy squeezed my fourth-grade breasts and ran away giggling. I felt shocked and ashamed. I already knew about my breasts; they were big enough to demand a bra, after all. But right then and there I started hating my body for being something that was growing without

---

* I've sworn off scales for the past twenty years. I used to know approximately what I weighed by how a pair of pants from the year 2000 fit me. Fifteen years later, those pants were in a suitcase that was stolen from a rental car in San Francisco while I was interviewing a heavy metal quilter, and it was like I lost my metabolic North Star.

** Not recently. No, not recently.

my permission. My body was supposed to <u>be</u> me, but instead it was happening <u>to</u> me. Parts of it stuck out so far into the world that it became other people's business. Nine years old is early to start hating your body. Eleven years old is early to put yourself on a diet and be too scared to get up from your desk, because you can feel that your period has escaped the cushiony frontiers of the maxipad you're sitting on, but you don't want to tie your Polo windbreaker around your waist because you might get blood on it.

In eighth grade, I was at some audition, and the casting director asked for everyone's measurements. I had no idea about mine, so the stage mother next to me whipped out her tape measure. I remember her consternation when she looked at the tape wrapped around my hips—she murmured, "That can't be right," and measured again. She reported my numbers with a southern compliment: "I never would have thought you were that big." In my children's theater travels, surrounded by perky sprites and their mothers, I felt Brobdingnagian.

And so, spoiler alert: I proudly manifested an eating disorder. Took me long enough—I didn't get there until the beginning of my senior year of high school. I guess all the soccer and dancing and stirrup leggings helped stave off this inevitability.

My mother was complicit in all this.

First of all, this was a woman who'd pray the rosary while doing abdominal crunches. She didn't do this publicly, but I "caught" her once, and it was a lesson in time management. I'm pretty sure she did Kegels during confession, too. Second of all, more than anyone else, my mom witnessed firsthand the anguish I'd feel when clothes didn't fit, the tears in dressing rooms when I was ten, and she'd assure me I wasn't fat, I was just "developing." So she supported all my weight-loss efforts. But she never criticized my body. She monitored me only once in my life when it came to eating: when I was pushing the limits of my Guess jeans, and she saw me eating peanut butter by the spoonful out of a jar, she said gently, "Honey, that has a lot of calories, you know." She herself ate very healthfully but really enjoyed food. She played tennis every chance she got, and I never heard her disparage her body. Why would she? She had a sick body.

When I decided to lose weight, she started walking with me, an hour a day, sometimes twice a day—always the same route in our hilly suburbs. We walked through rain and 1,000 percent humidity and snowstorms. We were like the US postal workers of low-impact exercise—nothing could keep us from the swift completion of our appointed rounds. While we walked, we talked about everything that ever happened, from her first boyfriend to sex to my dreams for the future. Once, as I was huffing my way up the steepest hill with my hands on the back of my waist and my elbows pointed behind me as if they were triangular propellers, she said, "I can't wait to see you walk like that when you're cute and pregnant." Getting pregnant was the furthest thing from my mind, but so was losing my walking partner.

It was on one of our walks that she doubled over in pain, and we learned hours later at the hospital that she had terminal cancer. Her body was now sick in a horrible way. We still walked during those last months until she couldn't walk anymore. Not for exercise but for resilience, as if clinging to this ritual could extend her finish line. I knew she'd die soon when she leaned on me for support. She'd always been my support.

I excelled at being anorexic. I navigated the borderline between skinny and skeletal. I didn't want to be hospitalized and taken away from my beloved musical theater gigs and AP English. I ate just enough (exactly eight hundred calories a day) to supply me with the energy to make it through two daily workouts, seven days a week. I lost ten pounds a month for five months and thrived on the feeling of hunger. Hunger was my high. Hunger tasted like triumph. I was finally in charge of my body. My body was my bitch. "Nothing tastes as good as being thin feels" used to ring so true. But I have found that when you're alone for the first time all day, standing in your kitchen at 8 p.m., watching the baby monitor like it's a reality show, it's arguable that candy-corn-flavored M&M's taste as good as thin feels.

Anorexia was my affliction and my vice—I didn't drink; I've never done drugs (not even pot—gives you the munchies); I wasn't having sex. I wasn't throwing up—that seemed so uncivilized. I was merely incredibly skinny with an insanely low resting heart rate. You could count my ribs, but you could also count on my GPA being irreproachable. As good as my grades were, my mind was unhealthy. Once I screamed at a navel orange for being too big. My parents had gone to visit one of my brothers in college, and they completely trusted me to take care of myself for a weekend, knowing full well I wasn't going to drink on my diet. Risky business for me would have been staying up too late to do a Jane Fonda workout on VHS. I discovered my father had left me with jumbo oranges. This unhinged me. I hurled one across the kitchen screaming "GOD DAMMIT!" at the oranges for being so swollen with extra calories and at my father for undermining the mission.

I liked hearing teachers whisper their worries to my parents. No one had ever been concerned about me, and it felt cozy to inspire anxiety about, say, the fact that my hands had turned orange due to my beta-carotene consumption. One night, during the spring of my senior year of high school, my father held me by the shoulders in our kitchen. Or maybe he just rested his fingertips in the well of my clavicle. We were standing next to the refrigerator. Tears choked his voice as he asked, "Why? Have I not told you enough that I think you're beautiful?" It felt like some small, weird victory, eliciting that kind of emotion from him.

My eating disorder gave me the edge. My college transfer application asked me to describe a book that had a meaningful impact on my life. I composed an essay about the *LeGette's Calorie Encyclopedia* that I'd kept in my bathroom for years and would pore over like it was a cliff-hanging classic. Harvard accepted me.

If it sounds like I'm romanticizing an eating disorder, I'm not. I wouldn't wish that sickness on anyone—it eats away at joy and swallows spontaneity. It camps out in your soul, taking up space that could be used to dream or love or rest. I do miss being able to wear anything, and I miss the clarity of purpose and the efficacy of effort. It was rigorous, but it was simple. Of course, what I've gained besides pounds is the bigger, more complicated life that I talked about during all those walks with my mom. My life used to be lean. Rigidity is necessarily part of my past, both in body and spirit.

Sometime in my midtwenties, my period returned like

a benign stalker. The pounds had crept back on—not that many, but when you've weighed in the double digits for years, you feel fat when you hit the triple digits. But I'd lost my enjoyment of the feeling of hunger. I needed the energy of calories to deal with things. My mother died. My marriage died. I eat when I'm unhappy; I don't eat when I fall in love. I was more unhappy than in love for a long time. My extreme willpower waned. In the same way that, after I left grad school, my reading was a steady magazine diet of *Self* and *In Touch* because I needed a break from Important Literature, I also spent a decade eating a lot of crap, like a re-tox from my previously clean diet. And so began years of loving myself for loathing food and other years of loathing myself for loving food.

Moving to New York, filling my brain with healthful fare, having to push myself through wind and sleet and snow, falling in love a few times with the Manhattan skyline as a backdrop, no longer possessing a car to serve as a mobile binge unit—all these things helped me think less about my body or think of it/myself (because they are interchangeable) with a hint of appreciation. But it was being pregnant that was the game changer.

I'll skip all the clichés about how pregnancy teaches you how strong and amazing your body is—clichés because they're true. I didn't get swollen ankles or varicose veins or stretch marks probably because I exercised every day of my pregnancies and probably also because I was very lucky. What being pregnant really taught me was to stop navel-gazing. I mean, I was totally navel-gazing, because I actually loved sitting in the bath watching my belly button slowly poke out of the water, while the rest of me stayed submerged, over the course of months. But I wasn't thinking about myself. For the first time in my life, my body belonged to someone else and that someone else had needs that were way more important than mine. Sometimes those needs were very explicit, such as an immediate demand for fried pickles. I ate lunch every day for the first time in decades. Before, lunch had been something to avoid, and my reward for skipping lunch was some dinner. Breakfast was something to eschew if I had to have a business lunch. Cheese was always to be shunned, as was fare like burgers, pizza, and fries and putting real sugar in decaf coffee. I gave up artificial sweeteners, prioritized protein and fat that sometimes appeared in the form of cheese, and allowed myself on occasion to eat fries since they were the ideal delivery system for ketchup, which became my primary food group. The big revelation was that none of it made me fat. Eating like a normal person was fun, even healthful.

I let my dear friend Sharon take pregnancy pictures of me, something I swore I'd never do. I love those pictures. I love my body in them, which is something I dare to say without feeling like I'm bragging, because my pregnancy body isn't my real body. They weren't taken so long ago, but I look at them now and think that woman in them was so innocent and young, even though she was forty-one. She looks so well rested.

Sometimes I try to imagine myself as an old lady— one of those tiny women with a tiny appetite. Birdlike, but without osteoporosis. Will there be a day when I can skip a workout without feeling guilty? Will there be a day when I just don't want to eat that much? Will I be young enough to enjoy it?

Not long before my mother died—after her last chemotherapy but before hospice—we went to a sunset dessert
buffet overlooking the ocean. We'd always shared a sweet
tooth, and we always sought to keep it in check. She was
wasting away, my mom, and, as we sampled a dozen cakes,
she sadly said to me, about all the calories we were consuming, "It doesn't matter anymore." I wonder when I will say,
"It doesn't matter anymore."

This chapter isn't really about my body or my diet. It's
about me. It's about how far I still have to go (How far? Six
miles in under an hour? Two hundred floors on the Step-
Mill?) when it comes to embodying gentleness. If a workout
isn't in some way punishing, I don't feel I've done enough.
Every so often, I should probably take a day to stretch gently, in more ways than one. That will be a day I allow myself
to be rather than push myself to become something more.

As I was finishing this book, I unearthed some old photos at my father's house. I found a few of me in which I'm
so bony that I'm hardly there. My husband glanced at them
and told me he was too disturbed to look again. I stared,
mesmerized but not disgusted. I remember that girl, but she
seems so far away. And then there's one of my mother, a decade after having her third child, standing on the beach in a
bikini. Her smile is wide; her strong, tan body is ridiculous.
Curves where they should be, concave where you want it. I
recall people often admiring her figure, but I never appreciated it through the eyes of the mother I am now. I don't own
a bikini or a tan, but maybe I should find the rosary she left
me and get crunching.

On this same visit to my dad's, I put my daughter in her
first bathing suit. It's a hot pink number with a massive

kind of Valentino knockoff rosette that draws attention to her huge belly. She was tramping around like an agile Sumo wrestler in Crocs, and I just wanted to tackle her to squeeze her pudgy, sturdy legs. I'm already sad that there will soon be a day when she loses the scrumptious cellulite on her butt and then there will be a day after that when the cellulite will likely return and she'll likely hate it.

I hope she is healthy, and I hope she is happy, and I hope she lets herself have more than the crust.

The Best Hand Job Ever

If you're wondering how my brother taught me how to give the best hand job ever, it all began in his Stanford Law torts class. I will render your worst fears flaccid by telling you now that no penises were involved. It was the year after Mom died, and David and I made it a point to visit each other once a month, since we were both in California. It was such a comfort to have my brother in my time zone and an hour flight away during those days. So I'd flown up on a Friday and gone with him to his lecture. I brought along some light reading on heavy petting.

I nestled the sex manual behind a large folder. The book was called *Sex Tips for Straight Women from a Gay Man*. It offers a solid premise—who better to teach you how to please a man than a man who pleases men? I was eager for sex tips because I'd recently started dating my wasband. From our first date, I just knew I wanted to marry him. It wasn't even because he told me he was going to be president of the United States, setting off FLOTUS fantasies in my head. It was because he was confident and tall and handsome. He had a deep, sexy voice. But there was also something vulnerable about him, because he'd been very sick for a very long time. How often do you get to be the first person with whom someone has sex after he finishes chemotherapy? That's Remission Sex. That's a big deal. I didn't want to let him down in any way.

Sex Tips for Straight Women from a Gay Man turned out to be more rompy than revelatory except for a few pointers. And by "pointers," I do mean nipples. Men's nipples, which, according to this primer, are lonely, evolutionarily impotent accessories just waiting to be noticed. I'm not so sure about this tip, as I have since attempted to lavish attention on the male nipples of a small sample set and haven't had any takers.*

The other surprising suggestion focused on the overlooked art of hand jobs. I hadn't thought about hand jobs in years. In fact, I don't think I'd ever actually thought about hand jobs, because what I was thinking during the three occasions in high school when I'd stuck my hand down a young man's pants was, *OH MY GOD I'M TOUCHING A*

---

* I've just conducted a study on this topic using the scientific method, which you probably remember from middle school involves texting both your gay brother and straight brother and asking, "Need to know: do most men like to have nipple action during sex? Thank you for your time."

Doug got back to me first: "Not my 'thing.' "

Then David: "I've always wondered about straight guys. Among the gays, it seems to be about 50/50. Half have 'wired nips,' and the other half, no particularly special sensation." Interestingly, David does not reveal himself to be wired or not. I will ask him during Thanksgiving dinner.

PENIS AND IT'S GETTING BIGGER. HOW MUCH BIG-GER WILL IT GET? NOW I THINK I'M A LITTLE AFRAID OF WHAT THIS PENIS AND GOD WILL DO TO ME.

But the book made a very enthusiastic argument for re-visiting the hand job, just as a gastronome might, once in a while, crave a Sloppy Joe. I was persuaded and hungry to try it out. Except first I had to fully understand the directions, which were surprisingly complex for this meat and potatoes move.

And that's why I was perched beside my brother in the stadium seating of his 2L Torts class, scrutinizing the con-fusing diagram entitled "The Stroke." According to the *Gay Man*, the key to The Stroke was a twisting move. I kept dis-creetly trying to mimic the pictures full of penises and ar-rows with one hand while holding up the book and folder with the other. I prayed the professor wouldn't call on me in a *Paper Chase* moment, leaving me no choice but to answer, "I haven't done the reading, sir, but I <u>can</u> speak to *manu forte* ejaculation techniques."

David noticed my furrowed brow, so I tilted the diagram at him. He quickly studied it and whispered, "I'll show you at home."

"It says to practice on a roll of refrigerated cookie dough," I whispered back, just to make sure he wasn't planning on whipping out his thang. I mean, we're close, but we're not that close. He nodded solemnly.

Perhaps it strikes you as weird that I asked my brother for help when it came to sex—even if he <u>is</u> the brother who knows his way (up and) around a penis. But you see, I can ask David anything. Although I will always regret asking who does what to whom in his sex life with his husband. To be clear: it's not gross because they're both men. It's a little gross because it's my brother. Kind of like when my sister-in-law, Lorei, and I took a pole dancing class together. (Yes, that's how you spell her name; just ask her sister, Carei.) We took turns practicing the lap dance while envisioning our lover in the empty chair. I seduced the chair after her, and my performance was completely ruined by the fact that, in Lorei's imagination, my oldest brother, Doug, had just been sitting there, possibly erect. Because he was invisible, I was afraid he/it was still there.

I can ask David anything, and I can ask anything of him. With the possible exception of my husband, I can say that as close as I've been with any man, I've been closer with my brother. John has seen me breastfeed thousands of times, but only with David have I frolicked topless on a beach. John has witnessed wee people come out of my magical lady hole, but David was with me while I had my uterus rearranged by a resectoscope loop to make room for a potential baby. John has watched me become a mother; David has seen me lose our mother.

My husband loves me patiently, but my brother has loved me longer. Even when he disapproved, my brother stayed beside me. When we fought in a Roman amphitheater in Arles the summer I was eighteen because he thought I was starving myself; when he strongly suggested, a month before my first wedding, that I not marry a man who had just fired me as a client because we'd argued about the wording of our *New York Times* wedding announcement—David stuck around. He held the train of my gown as I married my

wasband and never said "I told you so" when he flew from
DC to LA for twenty-four hours to help me pack up my life
during my divorce.

Men have come (and come again) and gone, but not my
brother. And so I asked him to teach me the twist.

Doesn't everyone, at one time or another, try to impress
in bed? Impressing in bed, though, often means doing it out
of bed. The most spectacular sex I've ever had—and I use
that word advisedly because, if anyone saw us, we created
a spectacle—was with a hot triathlete. Trip was so handsome that I always worried that people might look at us
and think, *What's he doing with _her_?*, so I really tried to up
my game. When we met, I actually had no game—he introduced me to a lot of creative ideas involving baby oil, a
waterbed, strawberries, the hood of his BMW, an elevator,
his mother's garden (*not* a euphemism), and a public botani-
cal garden. Not all at once.

Before Trip, I'd had sex with two people. Not all at once.
Seems to me there are a couple of ways to win approval
when it comes to sex: one is through having it lots of different ways and the other is by not having it at all. As a teenager, I chose the latter. I was a Very Good Girl. I was saving
myself, not out of some chipper Christian youth group commitment to chastity but out of a sense of honor. Of waiting
to meet someone worthy. Also, it didn't seem to fit into my
teetotaling, studying, early-to-bed, early-to-rise lifestyle. It's
hard to have casual—or formal—sex when the only crack
you want to see is of dawn so you can get in an early run.

I remember being in a college dressing room while playing Sandy in *Grease* and seeking advice from a castmate
about whether I should hold out until after I turned twenty

to have sex for the first time. This friend, while applying her dark red lipstick, said, "Oh God. I would <u>never</u> want to be a twenty-year-old virgin." Obviously, she played Rizzo.

I lost my virginity to my college boyfriend in a responsible encounter after months of dating and earnest professions of love. It was undramatic except for the fact of it. I called my mother the next morning to confess. I needed her to know. It wasn't so much that I was worried she might disapprove—after all, this was a lady who'd informed me on one of our walks that Astroglide was an excellent product and thought I should know that she and my father had "some kind of sex" almost daily. This was a woman who'd taught me, at age three, all the anatomically correct names of all the parts of the vulva and who'd recently sent me a Valentine's present of a red lace bra and thong. I'd never seen a thong up close before and therefore wore it backward for a day, giving myself a vagina wedgie. But she was still my mom, the person who thought I could do no wrong, and I just needed to make sure I was still never wrong. So I asked her if it was okay that I'd done . . . this thing. She was quiet and then asked me, "Do you really love him?" I assured her I did, and we both breathed a sigh of relief.

By the time Trip and I hooked up—and, yes "hooking up" is appropriately applied when you consider we met in front of the Leaning Tower of Pisa, learned we grew up a few miles apart, and then fell into bed because I'd finally started drinking at the age of twenty-four—I knew sex didn't have to mean being "really" in love. He taught me it could be purely fun. But for Trip, it would have never occurred to me to go out for the night *sans* panties. Or to do it sitting on his lap on the living room sofa, with a blanket draped over me, as we nonchalantly pretended to watch an NFL game when his mother, who was visiting, walked in. We pulled off a brief conversation about lunch with her while we scored a touchdown. More teamwork was to be had when he taught me how to harness the power of a Jacuzzi jet—a helpful skill I employed on my first honeymoon, when three out of three orgasms were provided by five-star hotel water fixtures.

Trip was the first man to ask me to touch myself in front of him. Now, I'd been giving myself hand jobs for years—ever since I invited fingers into my underwear at age eleven and got a surprise payoff—but I'd never considered doing this in <u>front</u> of someone, namely someone who was supposed to be giving me pleasure. I actually thought it might send a rude message to take matters into my own hands, like, "You clearly can't handle this as well as I can." But I tried it—I felt really self-conscious at first, to have an audience for something I'd only ever done alone. I started it for him, but I finished it for me. There was something sexy about knowing that watching me was giving him pleasure, but the sexiest part of all was just plain pleasing myself. A spiritual 69, if you will, which is an apt metaphor, since he's the one who first folded me into that numerical position.

Trip was really into videotaping sex and had amassed a small library of poignant encounters he never wanted to forget. I found it creepy but tried to chalk it up to his "porno-rakish charm." I told him never, noway, nohow with me—the only way I'd ever allow myself to be on camera naked would be if I did a thirty-day juice cleanse followed by a chaser of self-tanner. But one day, after amassing both mutual trust and masturbation, I relented. On one condition: no film in the camera. (If you are under thirty, there used to be such things as "cameras" that used "film." If you didn't have film in the camera, you didn't get to watch yourself! I know being unable to video yourself can be a terrifying thought, so let's all pause to make sure our smartphones are charged.) Apparently, just turning it on was enough to turn him on, and turning him on always worked out well for me.

I'd totally forgotten about the sex tape Trip and I didn't make until a few months later. My parents paid a visit to Trip's house, and he was showing us a video tour of his new Palm Beach condo. (Did I mention he was rich?) All of a sudden, while we were all sitting round the giant flat-screen, admiring his new closet space, an image of Trip having sex with some blond woman flashed before our eyes. (I'm not blond.) No one moved; no one said a word. I think we were all saying silent prayers that we'd individually experienced a weird subliminal porno that no one else saw. Almost immediately, the condo walk-through returned, and, as a group, we intently focused on the master suite. It was as if we were willing this incredibly boring home tour never to end, never to have its broadcast interrupted by a special report on boning. Alas, there was more breaking news about urgent boning, and once again—this time for several eternal seconds longer—my folks and I were treated to something more climactic than a Jack and Jill bathroom.

The triathlete fumbled the remote and, for all his athletic alacrity, seemed to take forever to block the screen and turn off the TV.

He didn't want to turn around. My mouth was open; my mother had one hand over her mouth and the other over her heart. My father saved the day. He said, simply, "Nice ass, Tripper."

For all his money, Trip had unwisely cut corners by reusing an old videotape.

It seemed that Trip had been the golden era of my sex life until I let someone pee on me. I wish I could tell you there was a jellyfish sting involved, but there wasn't.

During my first, temporary separation from the wasband, I started seeing someone. By "seeing someone," I mean I would meet this man at a motel every so often. (There's a huge difference between motels and hotels, and if you don't believe me, take a black light to the bedding.) This someone was a six-foot-five person with a cartoonishly massive jawline. He looked like Gaston from *Beauty and the Beast* if Gaston cut his ponytail and were approaching middle age. He was not so much affectionate as respectfully aggressive, which I found really hot since I was so hungry for sexual attention that I was in ketosis. We hardly kissed, and we didn't look into each other's eyes when we were having sex.

Gaston asked early on if he could pee on me, except he didn't say pee, he said "piss," as if that's sexier. Call it piss, pee-pee, or tinkle, nothing seemed sexy about it. I laughed, hoping he was joking, and gave him an incredulous "Uhhh, *nope.*" Meeting him in a motel was about as freaky as I wanted to get. It was the idea of our encounters that satisfied me. I was acting out of anger, under which was pain, under which was need—I was getting revenge on my wasband even though he knew nothing about it. If revenge falls in the forest, but your husband isn't around to hear it, is it still revenge? I dug feeling wanted, but I felt lonelier after every encounter, even when Gaston would leave sexy messages for me in the voice that had made him decent money speaking for video-game characters.

I kept hoping the carnality of it all might lead to the kind of sexual awakening you find in women's erotica. I was waiting for the toe-curling breakthrough. One night when I'd lubricated my prefrontal cortex with some wine, and my generous lover again offered to pee on me, the thought flitted across my brain that maybe I was being closed-minded. Maybe being peed on would make me some kind of sexual iconoclast. I said okay.

He escorted me gallantly in the dark to the shower and did his thing. It was blessedly quick and below the waist. I was frozen with grossed out-ness. He was, obviously, relieved.

Of all the things I've ever done for approval, this was the dumbest. It's not like it was on my bucket list, or even a bedpan list. I didn't grow as a person; I didn't learn anything new. Because getting peed on is like . . . getting peed on. It feels hot like pee and smells like pee. Because it's *urine*. It was all consensual, so I didn't feel degraded, just empty, which pretty much sums up how the whole affair left me feeling. And "affair" is misleading, since it connotes some kind of romance or passion. This was more of an experiment on my part to see if I could be a libertine. Turns out it's not my bag. Turns out I love to be wanted and treasured and wet but dry in all the right places.

In my experience, real intimacy is quiet, and it is cumulative. It doesn't arise from outré acts. It's made of moments when you're naked with your eyes open, and whether or not you have clothes on doesn't matter. I can count on one hand the men with whom I've been truly unblinking, and they with me, and my brother is one of them. My brother's eyes are open to my flaws and cracks, and he still loves me.

Intimacy is also spontaneous and organic. It's not something you need to study for, even if you find explicit instructions in a book, and even if you have a brother willing to explain them to you.

There's really no way of knowing if David and I are so close because he's my brother or he's my <u>gay</u> brother. It doesn't matter anyway; he's more than a brother and more than a best friend, and he's better than a sister. I didn't even know he was gay until he came out to me in our twenties over some Chick-fil-A at the Perimeter Mall food court. Had I a discerning eye for adolescent boy wall art, I might have registered that in my brother Doug's room hung the iconic poster of Farrah Fawcett in her nipply glory, while David's corkboard sported an 8 x 10 glossy of Joan Rivers.

When someone has sung the entire cast recording of *Les Mis* with you on a convertible road trip in 1987; when, years later, after your mother's death, he's walked with you beside the Pacific and talked about when it might feel okay to sing anything ever again; when you've asked him to buy you postsurgical granny panties and enormous thirsty pads the size of European pillow shams to put in them, it makes sense to ask this man to show you how to give the best hand job ever, even if he is your brother.

As we drove from his torts class to my hand job tutorial, I reminded David that the *Gay Man* said we should use cookie dough, because it has the right consistency. We agreed that the girth of the dough was aspirational. Plus my gay brother is <u>gay</u>, and no homosexual person worth his pink Himalayan sea salt keeps slice-and-bake cookie dough in his fridge. He said, "I think I have something at home that will work."

And so we sat at his kitchen table in his humble apartment

on a sunny February day in Palo Alto, and he showed me the twist using a roll of sundried tomato polenta. I have no memories of how my deployment of the twist went over (or under), but I'll always have the fond memory of sharing that special moment with David.

My brother has always, whenever I've needed it, given me a hand.

The Exorcism

By the time my wasband asked if I would consider undergoing an exorcism, we'd been married three months, which, to be fair, is probably long enough to start suspecting that you've wed the Bride of Satan. Sitting in his lounge chair that he'd upholstered in a Latrell Sprewell Knicks jersey, he told me he'd just watched an intense video on CNN showing an exorcism. Then he fairly casually added, "And I was wondering . . . would you ever consider having one?"

For a millisecond, it looked like he was about to smile. But he didn't. And I was about to laugh. But I didn't. I think he registered how outrageous the question was, but he committed to it because he meant it. He really wanted to know if I'd noodle over this dispossession thing. And I really wanted to please him—even surprise him—with my willingness to subject myself to such dramatic self-improvement. So I said, "Yeah . . . I'd consider it. Do you think I <u>need</u> one?"

He replied, "I don't know. Sometimes I think there's something dark inside you that you can't control. Maybe we could get rid of it."

I was weirdly comforted by the fact that my new husband chalked up most of my distasteful behavior to my being possessed by the devil himself. It was as if he saw the best in me, and my best self was haplessly caught in an evil stranglehold that made me do things like show up sullen to the party his network threw to celebrate his show that I wasn't on, as aggressively passive-aggressive as I could appear.

I was depressed, probably clinically so. This didn't feel like the situational sadness I'd felt when my mother died; this felt like numbing dejection. But not so numbing that I didn't cry a lot, usually after an interaction with my wasband on the rare occasions I saw him. He was working all hours, and when he wasn't, he didn't want to be together. This is not surprising, considering how dramatically I'd mope around our apartment. He kept telling me, "Do something—write a screenplay," but every idea I had was just a plotless premise with nowhere to go, which is how I felt about my life.

I felt bad that I felt sad. I was living ten blocks from the ocean in a land where it never rained. I was married to a man who was finally enjoying success in television. I was healthy and young (though I didn't realize how young I was); my family and friends loved me even if I'd distanced myself from them out of the shame of recently asking them to eat haggis at a Scottish wedding that hadn't launched a happy marriage. And though I desperately wanted more jobs, I didn't <u>have</u> to make much money, thanks to an inheritance from my mother—not so much that I was rich but enough to enable my wallowing for a while.

From the day I left for college until we put my mother in hospice, she'd written me a card a week, filled with comfortingly mundane updates on her life ("I weeded the ivy

for 4 hours today, and my quads are so sore!" or "I chewed
so much gum, finishing my term paper for my Comparative Religion seminar") and supportive thoughts on my life,
which she found relentlessly exciting ("I can't believe you
wore a bikini on *Married with Children*—you should write
this all down for a book someday!"). She always signed off
the same way: "I pray for your peace, purpose, and happiness. I love you, Mom XOX." I had none of those—no
peace, purpose, or happiness. And no Mom.

My therapist Fran didn't blame me or Lucifer. She suggested I try an antidepressant. I didn't want to. I'm not big
on drugs of any sort except when trying to make babies in
my tumbleweed-filled womb. I hardly ever took aspirin, not
to mention I'd only ever smoked a cigarette while onstage
as Sandy in *Grease* for the glorious "Tell me about it, stud"
moment. Plus, I wasn't sure how to thrive without making
things hard for myself, so stabilizing my serotonin with a pill
didn't seem punishing enough. My sister-in-law, Lorei, had
recently stayed at this Ayurvedic center and made me promise to try it before I hit the Wellbutrin. Ayurveda = ancient
Hindu medicine focused on balance. Me = desperate.

So I packed my unhappiness, journal, and noga pants—
pants in which I never did yoga—and flew to Sarasota,
Florida, for a week. I was off to undergo Panchakarma, a
cleansing of the body, mind, and consciousness. I was ready
to conquer "surrender." This would all take place in a two-
story complex in a strip mall on the Tamiami Trail. It was
not fancy—several treatment rooms that looked like Massage Envy went to India, a tiny kitchen with some stools
at the counter, and a large yoga room with old wall-to-wall
carpeting, off of which were a few small bedrooms for folks

like me, who were there to crush Enlightenment. I didn't explain much to my wasband, because I didn't know what to expect. I just told him—per what I'd read online—that I was going to this place where they do things like pour oil on your third eye, that I wouldn't be on e-mail or my phone, and I hoped I'd come back healthier.

A tiny woman named Light greeted me with a strong hug as soon as I arrived at the humble healing center. She ran the joint. She was a sprightly woman, always in purple, who looked like an Indian version of Diana Ross. Her jet black hair and completely unlined skin belied her age, which she proudly informed me was sixty. I started fantasizing that a few good colonics and some lentils might mean I'd never need Botox again. We chatted while I ate the "green soup" that I'd learn was a mainstay of the menu. It wasn't quite small talk—more like medium talk, since she and I both knew I was there for a life-changing experience. When her husband, Bryan, came into the kitchen, she introduced me as "Our goddess from the West Coast." Bryan was younger than Light, and he looked like a cross between Larry Bird and the guy who plays the sun in the Jimmy Dean sausage commercials. His bio explained that his passion was "Cross Fibre Massage combined with Rebirthing breath and Forgiveness Ritual." I didn't understand what this meant, nor did I understand the rather Germanic choices in capitalization, but I was ready to learn.

Every day began with yoga led by Light. Yoga class was small: Light and Faith (sounds like a bad three-camera sitcom) plus a wiry local named Jose, and Peter, a baby-faced trial lawyer in his fifties. I had a hard time picturing Peter intimidating someone in court, mostly because he giggled

like a ten-year-old every time Light mentioned the energy of
his "magic wand." When he tittered, I doubled down on the
gravity with which I focused on the pink waves emanating
from my "yoni." I was taking this seriously. Light explained
that we are all stars, here to give light and joy to others. Also
that we should visualize ourselves as butterflies. I was ready
to be a fucking unicorn to nail this Panchakarma.

After a starfruit breakfast (you are what you eat), it was
Colema Time. Colema is a brand name, I just learned. I
made this discovery by visiting the Colema website, which
features a gushing waterfall next to a woman's belly button
and a sun-dappled photo of grass declaring, in cursive, "Enemas made simple." There is also an American flag so you
know the patriotic provenance of your simple enema board.
Just in case you've been homophonic and mistaken Colema
for Kalimah, which refers to the fundamental texts of Islam.

Don't let the mellifluous name fool you: that's irrigation
through your anus, people. Every second of it was horrible.
I persevered only because I didn't want to disappoint the
healers by holding on to the contents of my colon. After all,
I was there to surrender all my shit. I never really grooved
with the mantra Light had given me for meditation, but I
created a mantra to get through Colema. It was, *Don't freak
or you'll only make it worse don't freak or you'll only make it
worse. . . .* What I remember clearly is that when it was over,
Light cheerily inspected the results and declared me worm-
free. Win. On day three I cried uncle on the enemas, because sesame oil was dripping out of me in yoga.

Tarpana followed Colema. As best as I could understand,
tarpana is a healing ceremony during which you experience
cathartic release and reconnection with your loved ones. In

practice, it was Light and Bryan giving me a massage, asking me questions the whole time. "Why do you think you're here?" "What are you afraid of?" This kind of sucked, because all you want to do when you get a massage is melt and wake up with the outline of the headrest on your forehead. I couldn't enjoy their four hands on me when I was trying to impress them with how deeply I could breathe from the base of my yoni while explaining to them the whole deal with my wasband. Light kept calling my wasband "Steve," which is entirely not his name. They encouraged me to forgive myself. And they pointed out that Steve and I chose each other karmically—that, no matter how I felt I was failing, Steve was getting something from our relationship.

I was certain I was making progress and not just because I was letting myself eat the ghee Light kept serving. Ghee is clarified butter, which I was ingesting only in the name of Enlightenment. In my journal, I was writing about shining my light and being a goddess, and I was spelling universe with a capital "U."

Then Janine got her hands on me. Literally. Janine was the sous healer to Light and Bryan and assisted in tarpana. She was about my age, with ebony skin and fierce energy. The closest I can come to describing her is to hope you are old enough or camp enough to summon the image of Debbie Allen as the dance martinet in *Fame*. You know, when she bangs her stick on the floor and says, "You want fame? Well, fame costs. And right here is where you start paying. *In sweat*." That was Janine; just subtract leg warmers and add a turban.

If only I'd recalled Debbie Allen's immortal words about sweat at the time, I could have escaped the first spiritual lashing. The room was hot, and I apologized for being sweaty. Janine replied, "Do you know anything about me? How old am I? Have I been married? Where was I born?" I didn't know if this was a test of psychic abilities I was supposed to be burgeoning, but I decided to go with, "No. I don't know about you." She said, "Right. You know nothing about me, and my opinion matters to you?" She went on to point out that she'd been hearing me talk a lot in terms of "shoulds"—what I should do. And that I wanted to do everything right, and I apologized when I think I don't. She told me to replace "should" with "I intend to." All I could think, but not dare utter, was, *I intend to not sweat anymore, Janine.*

For the rest of tarpana, I endeavored to kill it on the honesty front. While Light and Janine rubbed oil on me, I further detailed my dynamic with Steve, perfectly timing my confessions between dramatic breaths. I expressed how I felt fear about our marriage, my career, my future. The ladies asked me what made me happy and I mentioned how much I loved baking. They demanded that I close my eyes and bake Fear a castor oil cake. So I did. I mean, I told them I did, because I really did endeavor to imagine a Fear cake even though my Authentic Self wasn't buying it. They highly approved of my cake decoration: I informed them that I wrote, in inspired icing, "I am the Light."

Then they upped the ante. They encouraged me to yell at Fear to leave. I yelled. I hollered, "LEAVE! GO!" Fear was obviously still kicking back on a chaise longue in the corner of the room giving me the middle finger, because Janine said I was acting. *Of course* I was acting. But Jesus, how bad of an actor was I? Apparently, I'd left Hollywood and flown to a strip mall in Florida where I still couldn't get a gig.

As I continued to sweat without intention, Janine shed some edifying light on my relationship. I told her about the dream I'd had the night before: I was in a bathroom and I'd slammed the door on my wasband. I was screaming—not a high-pitched, word-filled scream, but a guttural roar, the stuff of a Katy Perry hit. And when I opened the door, there he was, brandishing a chair with the legs facing toward me, like a lion tamer. Janine asked if I deserved his criticism. I said I did, and she said that meant I was letting him tame me. The ladies assured me I didn't need to be tamed, that I didn't need to feel responsible for his anger. And then the epiphanous hits kept on coming. I realized I'd felt so neglected by my wasband and jealous of his success that I'd been using my depression to get his attention and rain on his parade. And we talked about my mom—how bereft I was when she died, because she'd given me constant love and approbation. She provided the mirror that reflected the best and brightest me. When Janine learned that my mom had died the year before my first date with my wasband, she asserted that I'd looked to him to be that mirror and love me unconditionally. I'd asked more of him than he could give. She wasn't wrong. For years, I'd been trying to ask for so little, but maybe I'd been asking for everything.

Just as I dared to hope again that I was hurtling toward a breakthrough that would make Light, Janine, Bryan, the Universe et al. proud, I received devastating news. At dinner, over some ghee-laced green soup, Peter reported that he'd had an out-of-body experience. Peter, the attorney who turned yoga into a dick joke. He wasn't even bragging; he was as tickled as he could be that this crazy shit had happened to him. I didn't think I could achieve out of body, but I did know I needed to attempt something more dramatic than a castor oil Fear cake.

I decided to do the Kaya Kalpa. The mysterious Kaya Kalpa, the Mt. Everest of Ayurvedic treatments. It promised rebirth. Lorei had done it and couldn't even describe what it was like except to say it was like childbirth. (With all due respect to my lovely sister-in-law, let me say here, now that I've given birth twice—once without an epidural—THAT IS A TOTAL LOAD OF STEAMING HORSE DOOKY.) She came to the Ayurvedic center the day before my Kaya Kalpa to visit and have a few treatments.

Naturally, I spent the night before my Kaya Kalpa trying to cram for it. I asked Lorei to tutor me. The most homework she could assign was to think about what I wanted to release. Ugh, that again. The whole Gulf Coast of Florida had to know by now that I was there to release Fear and Anger. Urgent performance anxiety set in. I had only one day left to reach Enlightenment.

I shouldn't have worried. What I released turned out to be more powerful than a thousand Colemas.

I put on my game face as I walked quietly into Kaya Kalpa. I was almost naked. Bryan and Janine performed the first stage—in a darkened room, they rubbed me up and down my entire body with some kind of clay. The clay felt warm in the beginning, but as it dried, it cooled and tightened on my skin. This was no tarpana Q&A; I remained silent as they guided me through some visualizations and breathing. They coached me to breathe so deeply and rhythmically that I felt like my body was buzzing. They ordered me to originate those breaths from my "root," which is yet another Ayurvedic way of saying "vagina." I don't know how long this lasted, but at some point they solemnly helped me off the table and escorted me into the next room, which was helpful, since I was totally dizzy.

Light waited for me in a large bathroom lit only by a few candles. Bryan left, and Janine and Light helped me undress completely. I could barely see the flower petals floating in a steaming bath. By then I was so cold and light-headed that the incredibly hot water felt soothing. But the heat began to overwhelm, and I was eager to sweat all over Janine. She and Light knelt beside the bath as they touched me. I don't recall what they said, all I know is that they gently prodded me toward whatever I wanted to let go. The physical sensations were so intense that my brain turned off. At some point, Janine asked simply, "What do you need to release?" Suddenly an answer came out of me, delivered by my throat, but not by my thought: "My mom."

And I started to sob.

This sadness escaped me. I'd thought this grief I'd been carrying around for almost a decade had become background noise, like a low-level tinnitus. Every so often little moments turned up the volume of the pain—at the holidays when I longed to smell one of Mom's two-story gingerbread houses or when I just wanted someone (her) to play with my hair. I feel sorry for my wasband who had to be my date to all those weddings during the open marriage season that began in our late twenties when I would inevitably cause some drama. I was envious of every bride—not because she had a groom but because she had a mother.

I was twenty-six when my mother died, the same age she was when her father died. In fact, her dad died a week before I was born. I was supposed to be named Joy, but Mom was so sad that she named me Faith. He died fairly suddenly, and she couldn't fly to his funeral because of all ten fetal pounds of me. She didn't talk much about her father. I remember asking her about Pop, as we called him, when I was maybe ten. She started to answer me and then left the room in tears, so I thought it best not to ask anymore, not to make Mom cry.

That I still had sadness to release about my mother may not surprise you—people can spend their whole lives clinging to their mourning.

Still, it surprised _me_. I'd arrived with a goal, and a presumptuous certainty about what ailed me and what I needed. Since my conscious thoughts spiraled around my wasband and my career, I figured my subconscious ones did, too. So I was startled to learn that it was my grief about Mom that needed liberating. I was relieved, too—the truth had escaped me in a moment I didn't have to gin up.

But what happened next shocked me.

Janine and Light were pushing me to release the pain. Deep down, beneath the genuine tears, I still felt a self-consciousness about what I was doing and a hope I was doing it right. They goaded me to yell. The yelling hadn't gone well before, when Fear was such a bumptious bitch, but now I had a second chance. So I started yelling through the sobs—I was yobbing. At this point I was full-on pissed. My body was burning, and my yoni-root vagina was heaving. I'd given them their answer, and I wanted them to leave me alone. If there was still pain in me, I wanted that motherfucker out out OUT. I let out a howl—a "HOW'S THIS, BITCHES?!!" howl—that felt like something in my brain had physically clicked loose. That's when—there's no other way to put it—*the exorcism happened.*

On the crest of the final yob, I felt the presence of my mother and my grandfather. Not like they were there as angelic guiding spirits watching over me. No: I actually felt my mother's pain as a young woman losing her dad. At the same time, I experienced Pop's sadness, manifested in cirrhosis of his liver, that drove him to his own early death. Like a lightning bolt, their respective griefs electrified me, flowed through my body and out. My cells surrendered not just my eight-year anguish but generations of theirs. This was not the result of a thought process. I wouldn't even call it a realization—that gives me some credit. I can't describe this as anything other than a *knowing*. I did not achieve it. I received it.

So this was the real inheritance from my mom. One I'm sure she never meant to bequeath. She had passed on her sadness to me, as her father had passed his to her. Somehow I knew it was finally gone—unearthed and, instead of being buried again, dispersed like a mist. Somehow I then understood that my mother's death didn't have to be the central story of my life. She meant no less to me if I could permit myself to be happy. Happiness did not diminish the loss.

Does this sound crazy? I've since learned there's actually science behind it. Researchers have discovered that memories of traumatic experiences can be passed from one generation to another through DNA. (I hope this does not mean that either of my children will genetically remember how I got felt up by Edward James Olmos in a margarita line after I interviewed him at Comic-Con.) And one more nutty detail, just to be the icing on the castor oil cake of it all: after the yob heard 'round the strip mall, both of my hands froze. I mean, they were seriously paralyzed. My fingers were splayed, and I couldn't move them at all. I started panicking—I had no idea what was happening, and I was terrified the price I paid for Enlightenment was to go through life looking like I had severe rheumatoid arthritis. I was crying to Light, "I can't move my hands, I can't move my hands!" She told me to make them dance. At that point, all my un-intellectual spirituality had been tapped, and I was back to overthinking. And what I was overthinking was, *WHAT THE FUCK HAVE YOU PEOPLE DONE TO MY HANDS???* Janine and Light held my hands and waved them in the air. I guess you could call it "dancing," if dancing looks like a stroke victim getting physical therapy from two women of color in caftans. Slowly, slowly, I began to be able to wiggle my fingers. Later Light told me I'd experienced "tetany," which is "the involuntary contraction of muscles." Even my body was temporarily shocked by what I'd released. Having survived tetany, I now think it sounds like a great celebrity baby name.

Since the Kaya Kalpa I've never mourned my mother the same way. I miss her every day. There are times when I profoundly miss her, like when my son picks up a photo of her and smiles and says her grandmother name, "Gigi." I weep for myself and I yearn for her. But I no longer experience that despair that feels like a dull knife is scraping my insides hollow. The misery that stifled me and made me angry at anyone who had a living mother has been flushed out like a simple, American-made enema.

A day after I returned from my Ayurvedic adventure, I whipped up some ghee. Even if Steve didn't detect my dramatic release of dark energy, I did surprise the hell out of him by eating butter. Three days after I returned, I prayed to God in a new way. It wasn't a prayer to fix things or bring me something I wanted. It was an "I completely give up" prayer. I got real with God and said, "I'm not doing this right. I'm nothing but unhappy trying to get what I want. Whatever you want me to do, I'll do it. Even if it's being a kindergarten teacher or a firefighter." I actually listed those two jobs as proof of my submission, because God knows I'd be so wrong for them both: I'm not patient enough to be the former, and I don't cook enough to be the latter. A month after I returned from the Ayurvedic center, I was strolling by the Christmas tree in Rockefeller Center, inhaling the very New York City scent of roasted chestnuts, on the way to an audition that would change my life. A year after I returned, I was living in that city, hosting a national public radio show. (God had been gentle in assigning me a new career.)

I didn't quite know it at the time, but I had been reborn. Steve didn't quite know it, but he'd exorcised me out of his life. And though it would take awhile, I was starting to possess myself.

Face for Radio

I never learned anything when I was talking.
Larry King

It was the mouse in my office that told me I'd arrived.

The mouse didn't actually speak, although that would have been awesome. It was the <u>fact</u> of the mouse, because it meant I was really living the public radio dream. I dug the grittiness, grassrootsiness of it all.

If, even a couple of years before, you would have told me I'd be living in Manhattan, hosting a national public radio show and some new thing called a "podcast"; if you'd told me I'd be happier to have a rodent in my office than I was to have once had my own parking spot on the NBC lot; if you'd told me I'd finally make it to Broadway—because our offices <u>were</u> on Broadway, where our hipster team shared office space with a low-budget law firm, one of whose clients left an indication of his satisfaction with their representation in the form of a fecal deposit we all had to step over one morning to get to our staff meeting; if you'd ever told me any of those things, I would have told you to shut up.

Shutting up is what I learned to do, and it changed my life.

An e-mail from an old acquaintance was the beginning of how radio killed the (wannabe) TV star. Her name was Marit, and the last time I'd seen her, we were acting in a college production of the play *The House of Blue Leaves*.

> *Hi Faith -*
>
> *I don't know if you remember me, but I was the Little Nun to your Bananas. Until last week, I was actually working at VH1 (it always gave me a kick to see you on one of the shows!). I just quit to go back to where I came from—public radio. A friend of mine is launching a new show, distributed by PRI, the folks behind* This American Life. *It's a comedy show, and right now we're trying to pick the brains of all the smartest comedians we know.*

I thought Marit was being very generous putting me in her brain-picking group. I'd been keeping myself sane while waiting for Hollywood to give me lines by scripting myself, appearing as a talking head on those ur-reality shows like *Best Week Ever* and *40 Most Awesomely Bad Dirrty Songs . . . Ever*, where my job was to make culturally meaningful observations about Britney Spears and the lyrics of "Whoomp! (There It Is)." I was also performing stand-up comedy alongside gals with names like Chelsea Handler and Sarah Silverman and Tig Notaro. They were so much better than I was: funny, confident, specific. People were always asking me what my "brand" was as a comedian—what made my voice unique?

I welcomed the chance to talk with Marit about something new. She explained they were looking for hosts, and did I know anyone in LA who might be good? My new marriage was on the rocks, and I'd always wanted to live in New York, so I Dick Cheneyed myself into consideration. Then I slept my way to a public radio career. Oh wait, that part's not true, but I wouldn't kick Ira Glass out of bed for eating spelt.

The show was called *Fair Game from PRI with Faith Salie*. There was my name, right there in the title, but the best part was that, suddenly, I had my own show that was <u>not</u> about me. I'd spent a decade trying to sell myself, but now I got to focus on the not-me—on politics and science and arts. I read books and saw plays and films and researched fascinating people. I got to ask them anything I wanted. (Except Nick Cannon, whose people told me before the interview began that I should not say the word *Mariah*.) No one had to ask me what my brand was, because public radio is its own brand. No one asked me to define my figurative voice since I now had a literal voice. And I found that voice by listening.

I'd always fancied myself a pretty good listener, not least because I did improv comedy. A big rule of improv is to pay attention to what the other players are saying—to use it so you can build on it. But that kind of listening, even as part of a team, is self-serving, because you're keeping your ears open until the moment you add your funny block to the fun tower your troupe is constructing. There's a huge difference between listening to help yourself seem funny or smart or right and listening to help someone express himself. I was also, when I started, more of a good questioner than listener.

I thought being fearless about making bold, droll inquiries meant I'd be a good interviewer.

I had a lot to learn.

So here are some things I learned about listening. Master these interviewing skills, and the world is your oyster—becoming a truly fine listener creates a kind of magic that makes people fall in love with you a little, because you're really helping them fall in love with themselves.

The following techniques work on everybody. Listening has made me a better friend, daughter, mother, and wife. If you treat your significant other like a guest you're interviewing, then the goal of your exchange is really to understand him or her. It's not to make your partner see things from your perspective. This one is really hard to do, because our exchanges with loved ones can become so emotional. Sure, there are still plenty of times when the closest I come to treating my husband like a guest is, "Welcome to the Faith Salie Show, please sit silently and allow me to be right!" But it's much more ingrained in me now to breathe respectfully through tense exchanges rather than huff until I can insert my point. I try, during such discussions, to say this to myself: *This is* his *story. I may not agree with it, but I can at least listen to it.* If you can just pretend that it's your "job" to help your partner to express him- or herself, you can really learn a lot. And s/he will be so surprised and appreciative not to be met with interruptions or hostility or self-interested persuasion that you might get your way after all.

These tips work on first dates and job interviews. They work with your mother-in-law and in the middle of a fight with your spouse. And definitely with famous people. I've gotten Robert Redford to recite poetry to me, Anthony Hopkins to sing to me, and Don Rickles to insult me, all because I dared to ask and listen. (I'd add that I got Russell Brand to flirt with me and Ryan Gosling to ravish me with his eyes, but those guys can't help themselves and would do that if I were Charlie Rose.)

Stop Listening Like a Girl

The executive producer of *Fair Game* was a woman named Kerrie who looked like she floated out of a Pre-Raphaelite painting wearing Converse sneakers. She was a couple of years older than I was and became my radio big sister. She knew she was hiring a radio rookie, but she trusted me. She taught me to trust myself. Not to try too hard. To talk to my audience like I was talking to a single friend. (By that I mean "one person" and not "a single friend" who's looking for a relationship, in which case I'd talk to that friend like this: "Freeze your eggs, and go to a public radio fund-raising mixer.") You know that line about making love to the camera? You really have to make love to the microphone. It's exquisitely sensitive. If you laugh loudly, you have to move back from the mic; you must gently work your lips around certain words so you don't "pop your P's." The mic picks up your gasp, your giggle, your breath. Respecting the mic works like technological Xanax—you really have to calm yourself down or you'll alienate your listener.

When I started *Fair Game*, my wasband and I agreed it would be a temporary thing that would be good for my career, which, after all, he was managing. I flew back and forth from New York to LA a couple of times a month to attempt mouth-to-mouth on our marriage. Whenever I'd return from a cross-country flight, I'd roll into a taping of the show supertired. Tellingly, that's when Kerrie always told me I did my best work. "You sound like you," she'd say. "You're too tired to think of what you sound like and whether you're doing a good job. And your voice gets lower."

I sounded girlier when I started out and not just because of my pitch. Here's a gender stereotype—a genderalization, if you will: when women listen, we tend to give a lot of audible affirmations to the speaker. Kerrie pointed this out to me about myself. Acknowledgments such as "uh-huh," "I *know*," "mm-hmmm," and "TOE-tully" all serve to express, "I'm listening, and I'm with you." And off-air, that can be a lovely impulse and handy on a drinks date, but it turns out to be really distracting. I had to learn to be judicious in giving voice to encouragement. The best way to let my guests know I was listening was not by making little listening orgasms (*"yes!"*) but by letting what they were saying lead organically to my next question.

Another thing ladies and gentlemen alike tend to do to prove how well we're listening is to interject "That happened to me, too!" and then launch into a tale of our own experience. It took me over a decade to stop telling people, upon learning that they'd lost a loved one, "Yeah, my mom died when I was twenty-six." We think we're building a bridge of sharing, but, most of the time, we're really putting up scaffolding over someone else's story and clambering all over it.

Fair Game helped teach me this restraint, because the show was "live to tape," which meant I needed to act as if there would be no time to edit and fix my mistakes. (In reality, there was a smidgen of time, but the producers had less than an hour to fix my mistakes before the show was sent out nationally.) I was "on the clock": I literally faced a clock with digital red numbers that stared me down, relentlessly reminding me how much time I had left during every interview. At first I hated that clock. Then I learned to love the clock; it instilled discipline in me. I wasn't there to trade stories; I was there to help someone tell a story.

You're Not That Fascinating

Well, of course you <u>are</u> when you're not conducting an interview. You know that, and I know that. But if you pretend this conversation is not about you, you will learn a lot more. In college, we'd roll our eyes at people who'd ask "flex questions." Those were the kinds of questions that didn't seek answers but rather sought to demonstrate the insight, acumen, and toolness of the questioner. The simpler and more direct your question is, the richer the response you'll most likely get. Sometimes a quiet and earnest "Why?" leads to the most revealing answers. I found that that simple query would knock many celebrities off their game—which is a very good thing. So many people—both famous and not— are used to talking about what they do and what they think, but they're rarely asked merely, "Why?"

I interviewed Minnie Driver as part of a retrospective on *Good Will Hunting*. She explained that making the film had been so uniquely fulfilling that she hadn't actually desired to watch the movie too many times over the years, because she feared tempering her memory of it. She described the experience as "precious." The way she said it was so whispery and lovely that my first instinct was to leave it there, precious as it was, unprobed. If she didn't want to watch the movie too often, perhaps she didn't want to say too much about it. But then I remembered it was my role to ask, "Why? Why was it precious?" And she told this story, seemingly for the first time, about how, during filming, Matt Damon, exhausted by being writer and star, had fallen asleep on the set. She didn't want to wake him to rehearse their pillow talk scene, so the crew set up the lights silently around him as he slept on the bed. When the director was ready to shoot, she gently whispered to Matt what they were doing, and he played the scene genuinely half asleep. It was an intimate story, shared with palpable pleasure, that let the audience feel like they'd learned a secret or almost had sex with Matt Damon. (Which I almost did, by the way, in college, when he and I hooked up on a pool table after a cast party for a show we were both in. But we didn't have any type of sex, because I was a virgin. And an idiot, obviously.)

You're Not That Funny

Now you, you're hilarious. You make me pee. But something I learned from radio is that if I'm going to interrupt someone to make a joke, it has to be a joke that is totally worth it. Otherwise you're interrupting someone's train of thought and forcing the audience's attention to come to a screeching halt. So it has to be a joke that will kill, like murder in the first degree, a joke with blood dripping off it and a Lifetime movie in the works in which the joke will be played by Eddie Cibrian.

When I first started *Fair Game*, I'd get really nervous about the interviews—especially the ones on the ISDN, which is a digital telephone line, which basically meant I couldn't see the person with whom I was speaking. I'd stand in a booth and wait for the Famous Person to get on the line and pray that he was having a good day and hadn't gotten stuck on the 405 on the way to talk to me. When I could connect by making eye contact and smiling, I always felt more confident. One of my very first interviews was with Weird Al Yankovic. I could hear my heart pounding in my headphones and not because he looked so sexy in "Like a Surgeon." It's amusing to me now, having interviewed people way more famous and weirder than Al, but in the beginning, I approached every exchange self-consciously. I wanted to be funny and to ask all the interesting questions I'd prepared. Soon enough that nervousness dissipated as I realized, to my great relief and personal edification, that I didn't need to be funny, and, while preparation is essential, the best questions come from focusing on what my guest was saying in that moment rather than running down a prepared checklist.

I didn't need to be interesting; I just needed to be interested.

When I took the pressure off myself and became comfortable with shining the spotlight on someone else, even the most famous person became someone I was there to help. I wanted to help him or her tell a story, and I wanted to help my audience learn something new. This role focused me. It also cured me of starstruckedness for life. Knowing how to interview people is a very democratizing skill: it doesn't matter if someone is famous or not, since everyone has a story you can unlock if you're willing to devote your energy to it.

I once spent a week testing to be one of the hosts of a daytime talk show. It's called "a chemistry test." The producers throw all the potential hosts in a room together with pitchers of water and fruit plates, and they take you into the studio in groups to see which assortment of humans might deliver ratings. It's an inhumane process designed to bring out the worst in everyone. Hungry personalities talk all over one another, trying to be funny and relevant. During one of those vocal gang bangs, the lot of us were supposed to be interviewing a popular African American chef of humble roots. I could just see that he had more of a story to tell than all the jokes the ladies were getting him to make about his meat. I waited for my moment and asked him what it was like to be a southern boy who liked to play in the kitchen while the other boys were playing football. He got serious and shared a moving story about how he learned to cook because his family never had enough money to put food on the table for all his siblings, and he wanted to help out by finding a way to stretch the vittles in the kitchen.

I didn't get the gig, but I got a good story.

Pretend It's Bedtime

Remember when you were a kid and you were being tucked in at night? The best thing to say if you didn't want your mom to leave you was, "Tell me a story."* When it comes down to it, we all just want to hear stories. Think of everyone

---

* If "tell me a story" didn't work, you could then try my son's ace in the hole when I'm tiptoeing out of my kids' room, "Mommy, wipe my tears away." What an adorable evil genius.

as someone with a story (or a hundred stories). Craft your questions to learn where she came from, what she remembers, what happened to her, what was her nadir, her epiphanous moment. And get specific. For example, instead of asking Gary Oldman a kind of broad, "What's it like to be famous?" question, I asked, "What is the strangest encounter with a fan you've ever had?" This led to a bizarre story about a young woman who came to his door to show him a tattoo sketch of him she was about to get on her breast. She wanted his signature right below her nipple. And he was gentlemanly enough to sign it. No need to swaddle a question in sophistication if saying, "Tell me a story about that . . ." will do.

Silence Is . . . Platinum

When your goal is to connect with someone, silence is a sound you can harness, even invite. When you're having a real conversation, silence is better than golden. Resist the urge to fill the void. This one is so very hard to do, but, just as an exercise, try to spell "A-W-K-W-A-R-D" at a measured pace in your head before saying anything the next time there's a pause in a conversation. People hate silence, and when they will do anything to avoid it, they sometimes become very vulnerable. Instead of thinking of yourself as a hostess at a dinner party who needs to keep the conversation going, imagine you're a midwife to a story. When I allowed a moment to suspend (and this could feel like an eternity), I would often be amazed at what an artist will reveal. The same holds true for your mother-in-law. Listen through the silence.

I was doing a story on what it's like to be a "first

gentleman"—a man married to a lady governor. As planned, I'd been talking to a former first gentleman about his experience as a political spouse, but when I veered from "the script" and I asked him simply, "Are you proud of your wife?," he surprised me by starting to cry. He surprised himself, too—for all his emotional maturity, he was still a dude, and he didn't want to cry. There was a long pause as he stopped talking, which he thought would stop his tears. My first instinct was to save him and pop the tension by making a joke or apologizing for getting too personal. I wondered if I was being disrespectful by allowing him to feel his feelings in front of me. But against all my "Make things better!" urges, I waited. I watched him struggle to express his love for his wife and his embarrassment over it.

He ended with, "Wow. You got me. I didn't see that coming. I am. So very proud of her. . . ." And then he shook his head because he couldn't get any more words out.

Sometimes people learn something about themselves when we unlock them with a question. Sometimes we learn that it's not the person experiencing strong feelings who's made uncomfortable by them—it's we who feel uncomfortable in the presence of their emotions.

Either way, the learning is a gift.

Be Daring

Here's a huge secret: almost everyone will tell you almost anything if you just ask.

I asked Michael Keaton if he ever thinks he sucks. I asked Bill Bradley if he'd ever been in therapy. I asked Joan Rivers if she'd ever think she was pretty enough. They answered.

(Yes, yes, and no.) I wasn't sure if I should ask Zach Galifi-
anakis why he used the word *faggot* repeatedly in a live show
I saw him perform while he was dressed in an Orphan Annie
costume. I truly didn't think he was homophobic, and he's
so wry, he could have responded in a way that made me look
like a humorless, literal liberal who didn't get his irony. But
I had to ask. It basically went like this:

"So, um, let's talk about the F word you used in your
show."

"You mean 'faggot'?" He cut to the chase.

"Oooh, yes. That's the one. You said it a lot. Why?"

He didn't skip a beat. "Oh God, because it's so stupid.
How stupid to say that word. How stupid to care if someone's gay. I look stupid—I mean I'm this fat guy in an Annie
suit being stupid and only stupid people are going to use
such a dumb word, you know?"

Having gotten that out of the way, he told a really interesting story about growing up Greek among some xeno-
phobes in North Carolina.

Now, being daring doesn't mean being audacious enough
to ask *anything*—because then it kind of becomes about you
again, as in, "Can you believe she asked that?!" I found the
only time my questions yielded little was when they were
glib: Joy Behar seemed offended when I asked if the chair
she used to guest host Larry King's show had old man smell.
Elizabeth Edwards didn't cotton to my query (with a nod to
Bill Clinton's "boxers or briefs" moment) about what kind
of PJs her husband wore. (In my defense, this was before the
National Enquirer introduced us to Rielle Hunter.)

Sometimes we are least daring with those who are closest to us. For all my interviewing experience, I'm afraid to

ask my father about my mother. Our exchanges don't always go well. My father is an honors graduate of the School of Hey, Not Talking About Things Will Make Them Less Painful, which is a school I would flunk. I want to know what Mom was like as a young mother and what did she do after we fell asleep and did she ever start menopause? He gets very quiet and sometimes seems almost angry when I ask about her. I know he's not really angry; he's sad, still sad, and annoyed at me for asking him to remember. Here's a phone call during my third trimester:

ME: Hi Dad, I have a question for you: did Mom have an epidural?

DAD: [*labored sigh*] I don't know, I don't think so.

ME: You don't know??

DAD: It wasn't really important for me to know. Maybe. She told me the nurses made fun of her for screaming that it hurt.

We ended the call quickly. *I* felt like screaming, not only at those nurses, but at my father. How does a man not know if his wife went through that kind of life-changing pain, even if the '70s sequestered him to the waiting room? I want him to help me understand my mother, which would help me understand myself. I'm disappointed he can't deliver me information that's gone forever.* I feel frustrated that I can't

---

* Strangely, however, he claims to remember the moment all his children were conceived: he once told me that he recalls bumping my

listen to what I want to hear, but I guess it's all too close with my dad.

Recently, while hosting a new podcast, I was asked by the producers if I'd interview John about becoming a father in his forties. We sat in a tiny booth, and I asked him simple questions, which he answered quietly. Sometimes he paused for a long time while he found his words. I didn't try to "help" by finishing his sentences for him. It might be my all-time favorite interview. Not because he told me that meeting me had inspired him to become a father years after he'd thought that ship had sailed. Not because he teared up when he remembered how old his own father had seemed in middle age. But because, in that moment, I was all his, and he was all mine in a way we forget to be, with no pressure of somewhere else to go or family business to sort or babysitter to be relieved.

I thought, if only life could be like this all the time, or at least more often. If only John and I could connect—intimately, honestly, and respectfully, but without earphones and a soundproof room. How many things do I not hear because of the frenzied pace of our lives? What can I learn when I make the time to listen?

---

mother's cervix three times in their evidently gymnastic sex life, and each time resulted in a child. The real question here is not why my father thinks that a good cervical bang makes a baby; the real question is why he shared this with me, this one unhelpful, gag-inducing memory I can never unknow.

Shrink Rapt

Tina the therapist and I had been working on my anger problem. The problem was, according to Tina, I didn't have enough anger. I needed to stop beating myself up for how my marriage went down. My therapist was telling me to stop taking so much responsibility. So I was trying to get *bull tinky*, which had been my mother's word for "mad."

I've always tried to impress my therapists. It's a challenge: When you first meet a therapist—as when you first meet anyone—you kind of want her to think you have your shit together. But then if you had your shit together, why would you be there? The way I solve this psycho-nundrum is to be so forthcoming and nondefensive about not having my shit together that I feel unassailable. I try to wow with perspicacity about my shortcomings. I enter a therapist's office like a self-aware Wild West psychological gunfighter with my hands up in the air. "Here are my problem areas, pardner." I want to surrender all my flaws before they can shoot me down with some keen observation of something unexpected that "we have to work on."

Tina was tough. I traveled downtown to see her for the better part of the year I finally got divorced. I usually like to laugh with the people in whom I confide my saddest stories, but Tina wasn't like that. She was serious and blunt and didn't engage in small talk. I pegged her for a no-nonsense lesbian until she once mentioned her husband in an uncharacteristically forthcoming moment. I wouldn't have chosen her for a friend, but I respected her.

Tina suggested to me that my wasband displayed characteristics of a specific personality disorder. Of course, I delved into research of this disorder. When I scanned the checklist of traits, I burst into tears of relief. It's probably what people with advanced but undiagnosed Lyme disease feel like when they finally learn that a fucking tick ruined their health: *there's a name for this.* Vastly more enlightening was the description of what it's like to be in a relationship with one of these special people. There I was, summarized in a few bullet points.

- Your involvement is characterized by an ever-increasing effort to gain approval.
- You have come to believe you are the only one with the problem.
- You continually doubt yourself since you rarely receive outside validation of what you are going through.
- The common feelings that . . . emerge for you are frustration, confusion, fear of confrontation, exhaustion, uncertainty of where you stand with him or her, inadequacy, neglect, disempowerment, alienation from family and friends.

I understood myself a lot more. I could begin to forgive myself.

During a window in our separation when my wasband decided he wanted me back, I had an appointment with Tina. "Look, he's a scorpion," she explained, as I wondered why she was suddenly referencing astrological signs. Before I could tell her he was a Capricorn, she continued: "Scorpions sting; it's their nature. You can't blame a scorpion for being a scorpion."

"Okaaaaaaay . . . ?" I said.

"If you want to stay married to him, I can teach you how to be a scorpion tamer," she said.

I really didn't want to be a scorpion tamer.

Tina was the first and only person in my life to tell me I ought to be good and mad. I gave her lots of reasons why I shouldn't be, what role I played in my toxic dynamic with my wasband, how I should be grateful for all I learned about myself. She wouldn't have it. "You're allowed to be angry. You deserve to be angry. You've been mistreated, and a healthy response to that is to be angry at someone other than yourself. Are you afraid of being angry?"

It had never occurred to me. My mother had never shown me how to be a rationally angry woman. Maybe that wasn't her responsibility, but it would have been helpful to have witnessed her getting mad at my father and hearing how a marital argument might play out and resolve. If my parents fought, they never did it in front of us. But surely she had to have gotten pissed at him, if only for all the secondhand smoke he blew into her life? On the rare occasion she would announce she was bull tinky, she never wanted to release

her anger, because it threatened to burst forth as tears. Or
she'd get really angry at herself for taking a wrong turn and
making me late for an audition or overbaking some cookies
and possibly emit a "Shit Mariah!" that would send her to
confession.

My father could have helped me out, too. I certainly
watched him get mad. There was the quiet mad, when he'd
speak in deliberate, low tones, at night in the dark living
room, punctuating his remarks by bobbing the small orange
circle of the lit cigarette he was holding. There was the loud
mad, when he'd raise both his voice and finger and waggle
the latter dramatically. He didn't yell much, which is probably why I hated it when he did. But I was not encouraged
to display such a spectrum of emotion. On the contrary, if
I began to fume or cry, he'd say, "Stop acting." I knew I
wasn't acting, but I also knew I didn't want to make him
madder. I didn't act out; I acted in, sliding down in a car seat
to pout, as I shut down tears. It became my habit to save my
noisy moments for the stage, where I was allowed to be a
drama queen.

I was always afraid of getting angry at my wasband.
Actually, the anger was always there; I was really afraid
of expressing it to him. I resented him for big things, like
not wanting to marry me. I resented him for littler things,
like inviting his mother on our vacations. When the dam of
my pent-up anger would inexorably burst forth, he would
achieve preternatural calm. The more upset I got, the quieter and steelier he became, reminding me that I was the
hysterical one. I hit him once. I was so short and he was
so tall; I was so upset and he was so cool—I made a fist

and pounded his chest. To his credit and not to his credit, he remained unmoved. He actually smiled. After I'd get angry, he'd go away from me—physically and emotionally. Our fights never brought us closer, because every outburst eroded us. He'd placidly warn me that I would regret this someday.

And so I did. Once we were separated, I regretted it all. I thought if I'd never been angry, if I'd only been transcendent in my love, if I'd only been grateful for all that I had rather than resentful about all that I had not, then I would have been lovable. My anger turned inward.

I'd been congratulating myself on recognizing all my missteps and bad choices. Could Tina be right—could healing be as simple as being righteously, outwardly angry?

I gave it a shot. I got pretty good at it. I stopped returning bellicose e-mails from the wasband and let my lawyer take over. When he threatened to sue me if I mentioned him to our mutual friends, I ignored him. I stayed away from the scorpion.

Anger can be galvanizing. It helped me to stop focusing on my past, wallowing. Instead of looking backward, I decided to look down, in the direction of my baby-making area. I was going to become a mother no matter who wasn't in my life.

I decided to get everything checked out, tests run, ovaries lubed, the works. I learned that I possessed an unusual uterus. A gigantic fibrous septum ran down the middle of it, creating an impossible environment to sustain a pregnancy. If my uterus were on TripAdvisor.com, the reviews from a blastocyst would have been bad:

ZERO STARS—cramped, inhospitable!!
Worse than a hostel—totally HOSTILE!! Also no Wi-Fi.

I had surgery to correct it. And then I started bleeding. No, not from <u>there</u>, you guys—that's too obvious. From *there*. Blood was coming out of my butt. I was in so much pain that I could only get off the toilet long enough to call my friend Hubert. It was Memorial Day weekend, but I knew he'd save me. Hubert is the clutchiest of friends. Hubert is a straight man of Taiwanese extraction who regularly encouraged me to see the Broadway musical *Mamma Mia!* He can recite pi out to fifty-one digits. Ice Hube came right over, got me in a taxi, and didn't bat an eye when I explained the situation in between gut-grabbing groans.

Turned out I had hemorrhagic colitis caused by antibiotics. My colon had managed to get extremely angry. I spent the entire holiday weekend in the ER in my own room, because my friend Alexis happened to be the attending doctor, and she wanted to keep an eye on me. The whole thing was serendipitous, except for the hemorrahaging part, because I'd long wanted to introduce Alexis and Hubert. It was a meet cute, sponsored by my colon. Unfortunately, there was no spark. I was sad about this, since I had a fantasy of toasting them at their wedding with, "I'm the asshole who brought these two together." But Alexis and I became even closer, probably because she had to put a gloved finger up my anus a few times.

Never one to shirk commitments even during an ER stay, I called Tina to let her know I was in the hospital, and I'd have to miss our scheduled appointment. I was giving her forty-eight hours' notice. She called me back and left a message letting me know that she had a paid cancellation policy, no exceptions. Feeling exceptional, I called her back. Clearly she misunderstood the situation. My colon is bleeding, I reminded her voice mail. She left me another voice mail, reiterating her policy. Unlike my bowels, Tina remained unmoved.

If I had to pay her, I decided I was going to show up for the session.

I recalled the family lore that my mother once put my brother Doug outside in the snow when he was eighteen months old, because she was furious at him. She made sure he was wearing a snowsuit, and she watched him through the window for a couple of minutes before bringing him inside. There were no witnesses, because my father was at work, and my brother David and I were just-born and not-yet-born, respectively. But Mom told us this story unapologetically, looking proud of her ability to have been angry and calm.

The day after I got discharged from the hospital, I dragged myself downtown. I sat in her compact, dark office, on top of the postsurgery sanitary napkin, on top of her sofa. She reiterated her no-cancellation policy, citing the fact that everyone thinks his or her reason for canceling is valid, and she didn't want to have to make value judgments about validity. She asked me how I was feeling.

I told her I was feeling lousy and exhausted. I told her I was surprised that she didn't demonstrate any flexibility in her cancellation policy and that I wouldn't mind if she made a value judgment about *bleeding from the butt*.

I ended with, "So, frankly, Tina, I'm angry."

That was the last time I saw a therapist. I'd like to think I made Tina proud.

My Summer Fling with Bill O'Reilly (or My Fair and Unbalanced Lady)

l had a thing with Bill O'Reilly once. It was years ago now, but how can I forget a connection with a six-foot-four-inch powerful man whose forehead made mine look dainty? We only saw each other twice, but I really thought we had something.

Bill and I met the usual way, as these things go in the slick, sexy, insatiable world of cable news: I caught his eye (my agent told his producers about me), and he wanted to meet me (his producers booked me on the show).

I was standing at the American Airlines gate at LAX waiting to board my flight back to New York when Adam called.

"Hi!" I'm always happy to hear from my agent.

"So . . . how would you like to go on Bill O'Reilly?" he inquired.

"You mean the show, not the man, right?"

"Yes," Adam said, rolling his eyes with his voice. "The show. *The Factor.*"

"Oh my God. When?"

"Soon."

I started laughing. This was a really big deal—I'd be talking to a famous host with huge ratings—and I was immediately thrilled. And nervous.

"Oh my God. Yes, okay, yes. Oh my God. Okay. Thank you!"

I hung up and only had to walk twenty steps to a bookstore to find O'Reilly's *A Bold Fresh Piece of Humanity*, which had been on the bestseller list for almost a year. I needed to prepare. This is what I do when I get nervous. I study. Before I date a man, I google him till I erode my manicure. Before I go on the number one cable news show, I scrutinize the host's memoir. It felt funny to sit on the plane, cracking open a book I'd never considered reading, much less purchasing. (I kept the receipt for a tax deduction.) I didn't want to be seen holding *Bold Fresh*, as it was popularly called—like a *Factor* fan shibboleth. I didn't want to be taken for an O'Reilly devotee, which was entirely unfair of me, because I didn't watch his show, and the only things I knew about him were:

· He is conservative
· He is bloviating
· He mixes up the words *falafel* and *loofah* when it comes to which one he'd like to apply genitally to a young woman

His book confirmed him to be a conservative bloviator, but one with a sense of humor, even about himself. There was something lovable in his self-aware swagger. I thought I could play with him on air. I marked up *Bold Fresh* with notes. That way, when we became the Benedick and Beatrice of Fox News, I'd be ready with references to his childhood that I could drop as bons mots to delight and flatter him: "So you're calling me 'Salie' now, O'Reilly? What am I—a running back for your Marist College football team?! What would Sister Mary Lurana think of that?!!" And we'd laugh and laugh.

I started watching Fox News in earnest, not just to catch Shepard Smith being campy. And I actually found O'Reilly to be the fairest of the 2009 Great American troika of Bill O'Reilly, Glenn Beck, and Sean Hannity. Which is like saying Randy Jones was the straightest Village Person. Beck and Hannity are one tricorn hat away from a 5150 hold, but O'Reilly said abortion wasn't a black-and-white issue. He didn't seem to hate Obama categorically. He even dared to offer, "I don't believe the republic will collapse if Larry marries Brendan." I ignored the fact that he liked to call Larry and Brendan "homosexuals" and thought gay marriage would lead to the legalization of polygamy. Basically, I invested way too soon. This was not unlike my behavior in high school, when I'd hear that some guy liked me. Someone who'd never crossed my mind. But now that <u>he</u> thought <u>I</u> was cute, I might find something in him to admire, like the way he drove a stick shift.

I boned up on *The No Spin Zone*. I identified O'Reilly's lovable quirks: he delivers his opinion in the third person—like "'Talking Points' believes that the president is over-reaching . . ." Sigh. That Bill is supersmart: by presenting his segments this way, they have a "this just in" feel, as if he's a neutral reporter of information. He reports; I decided to swoon.

I eagerly studied the way he interacted with "Kelly" (the beautiful and blond Megyn Kelly) and "Hoover" (President Hoover's great-granddaughter, Margaret. Who is pretty and blond). The flirtatious rapport those women achieved with him became my goal. But it would be much more of an achievement for me, because I was from the other side of the political tracks. For a public radio girl, he was a bad boy. He was a challenge. I didn't want to tame him, just surprise him. Papa Bear probably didn't think he could love a girl like me, but I was going to prove him wrong in front of a bunch of white people who like guns.

By the time I flung myself into Bill O'Reilly's TV arms, I should have known better: just months before, I'd spent a whole hour sitting on a stool next to Oprah, trying to woo her with my wit, wisdom, and shoes. I mean, y'all, these shoes—they are five-inch floral platforms. That description sounds hideous unless you're RuPaul's stylist, but trust me, they were Oprah-worthy. Astonishingly, she didn't comment on my shoes, but I can tell you this: Oprah shuffles onto her set in sweet flats (think Tory Burch) and announces to her colorfully dressed, giddy audience, "These are my walkin' shoes." At which point someone whose job it is to deliver her a pair of Louboutins appears, and she announces, "These are my sittin' shoes," and everyone giggles and cheers Oprah for sittin' in thousand-dollar shoes. I now see my mistake was that I wore my sittin' shoes for walkin', and once I sat, I had no more shoes for puttin' on.

Still, I made her laugh, encouraged her to tell a story about herself that made her tear up, and together we ganged up like girlfriends against the other guest on the show—who was a man-guest so, please, he totally didn't get where O and I were coming from. As we were walkin' out of the studio, my new friend Oprah calmly concluded: "That was good. That was fun," and four accompanying producers simultaneously sighed and smiled. Then the guards gave me back a Ziploc bag containing the two weapons they'd confiscated from me—a BlackBerry and a potentially deadly comb—and I slid into the stretch limo that was waiting, and what *I* knew for sure was that I'd get a second girl-date. I haven't seen O since. I didn't think I'd become her Gayle King, but I hoped I might emerge as one of her Favorite Things. Wouldn't you? Being a celebrity friend must make you feel special, because you have to figure lots of people want to be besties with a star, but the star plucked you from her orbit. It's like when you get the first class upgrade. You're suddenly a class apart from the hoi polloi in the economy line where you stood five seconds ago. And you've got hot nuts in your hand.

Which brings me to Bill O'Reilly. He wasn't going to notice my shoes. I was going for straight-up Irish Catholic–bred hetero chemistry. Even after the Oprah one-off—*especially* after the Oprah one-off—I wanted Bill to love me. This was a geographically desirable relationship. Fox News was just down the street, and, knowing full well his love of segments teeming with wordplay—like Dennis Miller's "Miller Time"—I imagined a recurring bit called "Gotta Have Faith." But most of all, this would be a career breakthrough. Being liked by the host of the number one show on FNC would demonstrate that I was intellectually nimble. That I wasn't a knee-jerk northeastern elitist lib; I was, deep down, a southern girl from public school who could play in a big philosophical sandbox.

Bill and I, we wouldn't sit it out. We'd dance.

At 10 a.m. on the morning of my taping, I received an e-mail from a producer named Ann telling me my topics (Sarah Palin and Michael Jackson's memorial service) and this:

> We are taping the show at 3 pm ET today and your hit time will be approx. 3:25 pm.

I had a "hit time." It sounded so breathless, so military. I furiously wrote jokes and e-mailed only the gist to the producers, hoping that Bill wouldn't read it ahead of time. Producers of news shows often want you to send them exactly what you're going to say so that your exchange has all the spontaneity of a scheduled C-section. This is particularly challenging if you're like me, and you know that you've been set up on a televised date as someone who is expected to deliver smart <u>and</u> funny. Funny often—at best, really—is unscripted. But when you've taken what little time you've been given to craft a joke, it can be challenging to deliver it when the person on whose show you're appearing happens to be famous for interrupting his guests. When you're interrupted midjoke, you end up not only sounding not-funny but not-smart as well, because you never even got to make a point or a joke. I prayed Bill would let me finish my sentences the way he let Dennis Miller finish his fresh material about Barney Frank's gayness.

Bill sent a car for me. I mean, Ann handled the details, but the fact that it was a gigantic black SUV made me think that Bill had something to do with it.

Ann, who was as cute as a southern button, escorted me to hair and makeup, and, within minutes, I looked like a Real Housewife. My hair went wide and my face went tan. My lips were shiny porn-star pink. I sat in the makeup chair, staring at my notes, trying to calm my nerves by memorizing jokes like a script. On most first dates, I rely on wine to help. But the Fox green room did not offer wine. What was offered, however, was Geraldo Rivera. He looked very dapper in a blazer with jeans—kind of like a Fox News sartorial mullet: business on top, party down below. He decided to give me advice.

GERALDO: Are you a comedian?

ME: Um, I guess that's one of the things I've been called. I try to be funny . . . but I also try to say things.

GERALDO: Comedians should never try to say things.

And with those parting words, they whizzed me to the studio. The first thing that hits you when you enter a television studio is the cold. It's always freezing, because the temperature is regulated for a hot-headed male in a suit, not a woman tottering in, wearing a tiny TV dress. I saw Bill from behind as he sat looking at his own notes. His head was huge. Then I saw him from the front as I carefully wiggled my bottom into a stool across a small table from him. He was formidable. He had the same makeup insta-tan I did. I could see lines on his face I'd never noticed on my DVR. He had pretty eyes. I had to break the ice.

"Hi, Bill, I'm Faith."

"Hi," he said, pleasantly enough, looking up from his notes.

He returned to his pages. He was all business; his mind was on the flow of the show.

"They've explained that we're gonna run a package of comedians talking about Palin, right? And then I'll introduce you?"

"Yes," was all I could muster, since I was shivering and someone was running a mic cord underneath my bra and raping my earhole with an earpiece.

"HI FAITH, CAN YOU HEAR ME?" boomed a producer, suddenly in my ear.

"Yep!" I said. I sounded fun, game, ready to go! My adrenaline was racing. I stopped shivering as the producers counted down for Bill to introduce "our" segment.

"It's 'Say-lee?'" Bill asked, almost conspiratorially, over the countdown.

"Exactly," I whispered. I was so touched that he'd check on how to pronounce my last name.

And we were off.

The segment was about six minutes. He interrupted me a ton and steamrolled over most of my beloved punch lines— although he did allow me to accuse Palin of delivering a speech that was like an Escher painting, which was a bad

move on both our parts, since prime-time cable is probably
not the place to drop your hilarious mathematical art jokes.
But in short, we were magic. His badgering forced me to
improvise. He got to do his thing, and I got to do my favorite
thing: *I made Bill O'Reilly laugh.*

"Good," he said when the cameras were off.

"Thanks, Bill, I had fun," I said as someone unraped my
ear and led me out of the studio.

I'd just speed dated in front of millions of people. I was
so high from my first date that I forgot a few of them were
sure to hate me.

The next morning I awoke to an in-box stuffed with
venom. Such as the e-mail from the gentleman who told me
that he couldn't believe the troops were fighting for people
like me and that I should be sent to the Middle East and
stoned and the one from the Christian lady who promised to
pray that evil would befall me. There was the one about me
being "a kunt on O'Riely." The worst, however, was the one
that said, "YOUR A FAT ASS." The cameras had shot me
from the bust up; but, still, that one sent me reeling for the
remote so that I could watch myself in slow motion to decide
whether the camera had added ten ass pounds.

Now the stakes were higher than ever. I wanted Bill to
ask me for a second date not just to prove to myself that he
saw something in me, but to prove it to the likes of them—
people who write that kind of [sic] hate mail.

Then Ann popped up in my in-box:

> *You were great! There will definitely be a next time—bill said
> he'd like to have you on again soon during our after-the-show
> meeting!! Yay! :)*

And a few days later, a producer named Ron e-mailed:

I wanted to talk to you about an opportunity to do something this week—to try out a format that Bill is thinking of making permanent starting in September. Let me know when there is a good time to talk.

Now, Ron. <u>Now</u> would be a good time to talk about doing something "permanent" with my new TV boyfriend. Ron explained to me that Bill wanted to start a new segment called "Dumbest Thing" in which I and another gal would bring to *The Factor* our nomination for the dumbest thing that happened that week. I said yes, I'd do it, albeit a little confused that Bill wanted to bring another woman into our relationship so soon. But I was willing to experiment with this format to keep our relationship fresh.

I received the topics. I learned that Bill was going to call Obama the Dumbest Thing for using an eleven-year-old girl as "a plant" in his recent town hall audience. I e-mailed back my talking points. What I didn't tell the producers, however, is that I'd spent part of the day on the phone with someone in the White House, confirming that the president had no prior knowledge of this girl or her question. I thought Bill would enjoy sparring with me when I surprised him with my research.

The big black car fetched me, and the hair and makeup team turned me into a well-dressed blow-up doll. I greeted the crew in the studio. I lubricated my earhole. This was old hat. I settled in across from Bill who was demonstrating a cozy familiarity with Juliet. She was tall and naturally tan and husky voiced. This will shock you, but she was blond.

The ménage commenced.

I didn't have much time to say anything now that *she* was dividing his attention; but I did ram in a decent, then-topical joke about vegan Heather Mills (formerly Lady Heather McCartney) needing more protein . . . and then waited patiently for my big reveal. At the end of the segment, when Bill proclaimed Obama as his Dumbest Thing, I ventured with a playful smile, "Bill. Obama is a great talker—he doesn't need a kid as a crutch. I spoke to someone at the White House Press Office today who assured me that the president had no idea this girl was going to ask that question. . . ."

Suddenly the fast-paced segment was in slow motion. I was waiting for Bill to smile back. He didn't. He squinted his eyes and, for a split second, I could swear I saw anger. Then he recovered, and, with a coolness, said, "And you believe that? No wonder your name is *Faith*."

He made my name sound like a dirty word.

Juliet laughed. The crew laughed. Cut to commercial. Cut to the core.

I overshot. You shouldn't overshoot a Big Shot. He didn't look up as I exited.

I was the Dumbest Thing. I'd been eager to prove I was connected, a bona fide journalist. But O'Reilly had introduced me as "a social observer," and I should have stuck to the script and made some jokes that would be aborted by interruptions.

Although the producers had checked my availability for the next month, I never heard from them again. My agent called and was told they didn't need me. I moved on that summer, little by little. I canceled my *Factor* season pass. I put *Bold Fresh* in the reading-recycling bin of my building. I stopped saving a certain Diane von Furstenberg wrap dress for the next time Bill would see me.

I meet famous people all the time because of what I do. And what I do most of the time is interview them. I'm not nervous, because I'm putting the spotlight on them. That dynamic finally suits me after years of trying to put it on myself, because I realize that I look my best in dim lighting. But being on Oprah's show and then O'Reilly's, I'd let some of the sangfroid I'd developed, the quiet confidence in my own voice, abandon me. I had a huge stage and a minimal amount of time to make an impact. I made the mistake of focusing on how much I wanted out of the experience instead of experiencing it.

Bill O'Reilly is a smart man. In fact, he's so smart that he's smart enough not to mention hardly ever that he went to Harvard, which would obviously discredit him in the eyes of his viewers. Bill O'Reilly is so smart that he could see that we weren't meant to be. He cut me loose before I got in too deep.

I, on the other hand, did my please-love-me thing. But at some point we all must—in order to be happy—give up trying to get a Papa Bear hug from an audience who will never fall for us. Maybe it's the in-laws or the head of HR at work, or maybe it's a bunch of viewers who think there should be a draft for the war on the War on Christmas. Still, I'm not sorry I tried. I *danced*, goddammit, just like the Lee Ann Womack song wants us to.

Even if dancing is pointless in the No Spin Zone.

What l Wore to My Divorce

"Inevitable."

My best male girlfriend Manfred whispered that single word when he saw me emerge from a dressing room in the Beverly Hills Saks Fifth Avenue Bridal Salon. It was the first wedding dress I ever tried on in front of only one friend. All the hoopla around gown shopping only highlighted for me the absence of my mother. I wanted just Manfred with me, because he said things like, "Inevitable."

It was an ivory silk Elizabeth Fillmore "Guinevere" with ethereal gauntlet sleeves. This was 2004, so I like to think I was way ahead of the *Game of Thrones* fashion curve. We were getting married in Rosslyn Chapel in Scotland—a place some believe once sheltered the Holy Grail—so the romantic, vaguely medieval lines seemed to make this dress The One.

Five years later, I was trying on dresses to wear to divorce the man who turned out not to be The One.

By the time I was preparing to walk down another aisle,

this time in the LA County Superior Court, I was done feeling sad about the end of our marriage. I felt defiant. My
wasband's refusal to sign some paperwork that would have
simply ended our marriage induced us to have to stand in
front of a judge to do the honors. My lawyer, who was one
monocle away from looking exactly like Teddy Roosevelt,
assured me that our case would be an uncomplicated affair.
After all, we'd never shared any property or bank accounts—
not even a phone number or mailing address. We never registered for anything except Crate and Barrel gift cards that
we split as soon as we separated. I let him have the personal-
ized porcelain bowl given to us by Lorne Michaels that was
inscribed with the wrong wedding date. I also let him have
the title "Petitioner" on the divorce papers, even though I
was the one who finally filed the papers two years after he
told me he didn't want to be married to me anymore. It was
very important to him that he be the Petitioner and I be the
Respondent, which makes it all sound like a light S&M role-
playing game. It kind of was, emotionally.

    As righteous and sassy as I felt, though, I still wanted
to look pretty. Just because I was angry and didn't want to
be married to him anymore didn't mean I'd stopped caring what he thought. This realization frustrated me, but ultimately I embraced it with compassion for myself: I was
ready to be over him but I wasn't quite. I welcomed the
gigantic nudge I was about to get from the legal system. I
knew myself well enough to anticipate that being in his presence for the first time in ten months would yank my heart
and quicken my pulse. That sounds passionate, but it's not
the stuff of romance novels; it's the stuff of corrosive karma.
Despite my lawyer's promise of no drama, I didn't know

what to expect in court—what I would say or feel, what the wasband wouldn't say or wouldn't feel. My literal appearance was the only thing I could control about my court appearance. It was a relief to focus on something as superficial as a dress after years of addressing deeper concerns. It felt good to dig into my closet rather than my soul.

I was flying in from New York to get divorced—something about that sounded very sophisticated, a bit Auntie Mame meets Carrie Bradshaw, and I wanted to dress the part. I wanted to look like a New Yorker, whatever that might mean, since I usually find black too predictable. To me, looking like a New Yorker would say, "You may have known me for ten years, but look who I am now, without you, *beyond* you." I further envisioned a look that said, "Yo, THIS is what you'll be missing . . . even though you've introduced your new girlfriend to our mutual friends, and she's a decade younger than I am and is also a fit model." I wasn't sure what a fit model was, so that gave me a massive excuse to google the shit out of this ~~girl~~ ~~woman~~ no, girl. After ferreting out her last name from my friend Hubert (Hubert, if you're reading this, I'm still not sure why I didn't get sole custody of you in the divorce), I applied myself like an Internet-age Harriet the Spy. The girlfriend was beautiful and blond and skinny—or, rather, perfectly proportioned, which is apparently what defines a fit model. She looked like someone who skipped the burn when she went in the sun and ended up with a golden tan in two hours. I could tell her hair never got frizzy in humidity. And, according to her photos online, she also enjoyed riding her bike in a bikini with no helmet. Clearly, they were having mind-blowing sex.

Obviously I had to look phenomenally proportional, since tan is out of the question for me.

For weeks I ran through a mental inventory of my closet. Did I want to wear something new—to christen it and forever make it The Divorce Dress? Should I hit Zara and buy something that looks good but is disposable—or was that too much of a metaphor for our marriage? I thought of choosing a reliable favorite, but I didn't want to put any juju on it. Reiss dresses are too expensive to smudge with sage.

Whenever I told women—friends or acquaintances— that I had to go to divorce court, they'd invariably, without skipping a beat, ask, "What are you going to wear?" It was like instant female solidarity: *of course* it mattered what I was going to wear. I was even in a business meeting pitching a TV show, and the subject of marriage—and my divorce— came up. The executive became very concerned about what I was going to wear, and we launched into a solid ten minutes discussing what kind of pantsuit might say "Hot and Feminine" instead of "Running for Office."

I solicited suggestions.

I heard "classic," and "powerful," and "sexy, but not like you're trying too hard." So . . . not slutty sexy but power sexy. I felt drawn to the Black Halo "Jackie O" dress I'd bought to appear on *The O'Reilly Factor*. Very tight, precisely ruched indigo denim—dark but not black, posh but tough. I'd already taken on an intractable man in that dress!

My brothers chimed in. Doug texted me: "Not cheap LA very classy NY. Sexy but smart, like Law and Order! Step out of court often to take calls." David's text read: "Something fabulous, Sex and the City, maybe red! Great hair."

For my kin, television shows spawned in the '90s were the new black.

Divorce court seemed to inspire in my girlfriends 1940s-era fashion fantasies, not only for me, but for themselves. Jo, a producer, cast me as a noir heroine and insisted I stand in front of the judge with my face covered dramatically in a black veil. And nothing was going to stop my actor girlfriends Kathleen, Julie Ann, and April from buying enormous hats and long gloves and smoldering in the back of the courtroom ... except that Kathleen and Julie Ann had to drop their kids off at school that morning, and April had to stand in for Jenna Elfman.

The night before my flight found me trying on one outfit after another, keeping on the same pair of pumps and throwing dresses on the bed. The sight of myself balancing in heels while struggling to zip up a snug sheath called to mind one of those rom-com montages where the heroine tries on piles of clothes in front of her girlfriends to boppy music. My scene was exactly like that—if it were Opposite Day—because I was alone and without a soundtrack. I certainly had girlfriends who'd have come over and spent an evening happily opining on my divorce trousseau, but I didn't ask. Any girly giddiness about playing dress up evaporated as I faced reality. I was packing a suitcase to dissolve a marriage I'd vowed would last all the days of my life.

In the end—at the end—here's what I wore: a Nanette Lepore silk dress with a black, tan, and purple pattern that simultaneously evokes leopard print and peacock feathers—an appropriate, yin-yang combination. It was classy and feminine. It had pockets that I felt lent an air of casual insouciance I didn't possess. I'd worn this dress just once before on a fairly recent date to the gastromecca The French Laundry, so I could imagine it smelled soothingly of lavender and sinfully expensive truffles. But what was most remarkable about this dress is that I'd bought it almost a year earlier, at a sample sale on a cold fall evening in Manhattan. Just after leaving the sale, my wasband had called me and made some kind of legal threat regarding our divorce proceedings. And, walking through Times Square, laden with bags of beautiful, deeply discounted clothes, holding the phone to my ear, it occurred to me I could hang up on him. I'd never done this before. I did it. I hung up. I just hung up, and he called back repeatedly, and I never answered. And the world kept spinning, and the neon lights in Times Square didn't even flicker.

That was the provenance of my divorce dress. The accessories were easy to choose. I donned my mom's gold cross as if it offered some kind of armor; Great-Grandmother Hattie's* century-old engagement ring, because (a) she was rumored to have been a tough old broad and (b) it fit me, unlike the engagement ring from my wasband, which we'd never gotten sized; and beige patent heels that echoed down the municipal hallway in time with my pounding heart. My toenails were painted "Modern Girl" and my fingertips "Starter Wife."

I wanted even more subtext. My friend Brian had strongly lobbied for my wearing "a G-string. And only a G-string." Instead, I went with hot pink lace Hanky Pankys

---

* Great-Grandmother Hattie did things like reportedly employ a wet nurse for my grandfather until he was five. He would come home from kindergarten and announce he was thirsty. (Sorry—you totally didn't see that coming. I'll give you a moment to shake your brain out.)

with purple hearts. I told my brother David about them, to which he replied, "You deserve a purple heart for surviving that relationship." I felt triumphant that this was a pair of panties that my wasband had never seen and never would see. A pair I imagined a future man might happily remove from my person.

I cared about the jewelry and the shoes and the nail polish and the underwear because I cared about those things on my wedding day, too. Although I had to remove my unmentionables at the last minute before heading to the chapel, since my bridesmaids agreed that visible panty lines threatened to take down the whole Guinevere look. Sharon, who photographs *all* my weddings, captured a shot of my flower girls looking curiously at all the ladies who are looking curiously at my crotch.

On a meaningful day, everything you wear can have meaning. It becomes what I wore That Day, whether that day is a beginning or an end.

My wasband and I saw each other from about fifty feet away. I was walking toward the courtroom, and he was pacing outside. There was a sudden recognition of each other. He looked strong and boyishly handsome, as he always did. I caught my breath, seeing him, the man I'd walked toward four years earlier, under a Gothic nave, during a glorious cloud break in June. The sun had streamed through the stained glass, and I remember trying to slow down—the aisle wasn't long enough to hold the moment as we held each other's gaze. He'd blinked his eyes so hard, as if his own tears surprised him, when he saw me for the first time in my wedding dress. My eyes were veiled in a blusher, and for once I was the less transparent one. I remember thinking, in that moment, *Some day I will tell our children how their father looked at me on this day.*

But on This Day, this day in the hallway of the eighth floor of the Superior Court, under fluorescent lighting, the father of the kids we never ended up having looked at me for less than a full second. He looked at me by accident really, and then corrected himself by turning on his heels and sitting himself inside the courtroom where he studied his iPad with intense concentration until our judge arrived.

After that momentary identification—for the next forty-five minutes—despite my turning around and pushing my chair back and conspicuously contorting myself, he never looked my way again. I wanted to give him a small, sad smile, the kind where the corners of your mouth turn down. Some kind of respectful closure for the years we'd spent failing to love each other properly. A decade-long failure deserves more ceremony than the judge matter-of-factly declaring our marriage dissolved. I wanted to tell him, with my eyes, that I'd loved him and I was sorry we didn't make it, but I never got the chance.

After all that time and energy I'd put into deciding how I should look, I never really wondered if he <u>would</u> look. Ironic, maybe. Or . . . *inevitable.*

Years later, I feel silly that I cared so much. I guess that's the distance of age plus fulfillment. I wish I could go back and sit on the sleigh bed of the furnished apartment I rented on West End Avenue and talk to that ~~girl~~ woman who was standing in front of a full-length mirror trying on dress after dress. I would tell her that what seems to fit now may not

suit her at all a season hence. That she will outgrow old fa-
vorites and slip effortlessly into something new . . . that will
fit her like a love.

I might also tell her—if she would believe me—that
one night, just two years into the future, she will be lying
in bed. She'll be in bed early because she's finally, successfully pregnant with her first child at the end of her first trimester. And she'll be feeling gross and exhausted and will
glance at the back page of a magazine she's flipping through
to put her to sleep. She'll barely register that it's an ad for
Naked Juice featuring a fit young lady out for a run. She will
sleepily think, *Oh I miss running, which my fertility doctor has
ixnayed . . . oh juice has too many calories even when you're
pregnant. . . .* Then she will do a slo-mo double take and notice that the runner is her wasband's girlfriend. And she will
feel so happy that she can't run and she is forty years old and
won't fit into any of her dresses for a while.

JSAP

In the early days of dating my husband John, I went to LA to shoot a pilot. Though I'd just put my thirty-nine-year-old eggs on ice, I was playing the mother of a teenager, who was really a twenty-two-year-old with a receding hairline. I sat on my BlackBerry while filming a long dinner table exchange and kept texting John in between shots, in between my legs. The creator of the pilot was Danny, who is a mad genius, simultaneously possessing the sweetest character and the darkest sense of humor you'll ever encounter. He also happens to have written Seinfeld's "Festivus" episode as well as my favorite line I've ever gotten to utter. In this dinner scene, my "son" asks me if I have cancer. Thrilled, I respond with, "No, sweetie—why? Do I look thin?" I'd filled Danny in on my dating status, and, in describing my new boyfriend, I'd mentioned John was Jewish. All my surreptitious texting did not escape Danny's notice. He announced to the cast and crew that I was engaged in "The Jewish Semen Acquisition Project," or "JSAP." At any given

time during the weeklong shoot, he took to yelling, "JSAP
ASAP!!!"

It was a long, Gentile-strewn road that led me to the
JSAP. Here are a few stops along the way during the year
leading up to the Project's initiation.

I Joined Al-Anon

Sort of. I don't know how you "officially" join, but I did go
to a couple of meetings in two different church basements. I
brought my own decaf, because I assumed there would only
be regular coffee served. I figured that people who want
to remain anonymous are not people who feel like adding
caffeine withdrawal to their challenges. I never shared anything, never stood up and said my name so I could hear a
chorus of "Hi Faith!"s. I sat in the back and listened.

Going to Al-Anon seemed like the right thing to do, or
at least the "it couldn't hurt" thing to do, since I was in love
with an alcoholic. My girlfriend who's an AA devotee kept
encouraging me to help the man I'd been seeing—and seeing
get drunker and drunker—for going on two years. A large
part of me hated being told I could fix this. I was figuring
out my own stuff—the direction of my career after my radio
show was canceled, how I was going to become a mother,
whether I would ever stop subletting other women's apart-
ments and living among their things, like old scrunchies, expired diaphragms, and a box with wigs in it, labeled "Dead
Girl." Committing myself to helping someone who didn't
want to be helped seemed like an awful lot to take on. And
perhaps a foolish endeavor, too.

He was a good person. Funny and generous. Self-loathing and self-medicating. He stuck by me during my separation and divorce. He cared about my family. I was grateful to him for his patience, for making me laugh, for introducing me to the nooks of New York, like the hole-in-the-wall restaurant in Chinatown where they let you bring your own wine. We kissed at midnight on top of the Empire State Building. Holding hands in Central Park, he taught me to notice the little numbers painted on lampposts that tell you what cross street you're near. I loved him when he wasn't drunk. I was disappointed when he was, which ended up being every night we were together. He was quick to leave apology notes on mornings after passing out on the sofa long after I went to bed. "Your boyfriend's an asshole who loves you—sorry I never made it to bed last night." I persuaded myself his Post-its were a kind of taking responsibility for his actions.

Our relationship was like the negative image of my marriage. Instead of being the one always coming up short, the apologizer, I was now the one with my shit together, the apologized *to*. For a short time, I confess it felt refreshing; then, for a long time, it felt burdensome. I was in a position of power I didn't really want, but I really wanted to use it for good.

It took me a long time to deem him an alcoholic. We didn't live together, for one thing, so I could pretend it wasn't always that bad. Plus, I wanted to be wrong, so when he told me I was wrong, I wanted him to be right. I'd never been close to anyone with a substance abuse problem before, unless I count myself with Crystal Light. I'd invested so much and didn't want another relationship to fail. But he started to turn belligerent when drunk. He got angry with me for not ordering a glass of wine when we went out to dinner. I took a swig of his coffee one morning, and it tasted like Bailey's with a splash of caffeine.

This is my story and not his, so I'll abstain from any more details except to say that a real turning point came when, gin martini in hand, he yelled at me in a hotel lobby about how unfair *Jersey Shore* was to the beach-dwelling denizens of the Garden State.

As is my wont, I tried to approach the situation with a checklist of Things I Should Do, so that's when I called my AA girlfriend. She suggested I race-walk over to my local Al-Anon meeting.

I learned a huge lesson from my two Al-Anon meetings. I learned that I didn't want to earn an Al-Anon token for attendance. Because the meetings made me sad. Sad for the people who were there—daughters, sisters, husbands of alcoholics, who felt stuck in relationships that caused them despair. Being in those relationships was not their fault. But I realized that I was <u>not</u> stuck in a relationship. I *would* be if I married my boyfriend. If I married him, I'd be signing up for his addiction, and I'd have only myself to blame.

I left with my own Serenity Prayer:

God, grant me the serenity to accept being alone,
The courage to quite possibly be a single mother by choice,
And the wisdom to not get into another shitty marriage.

A few months later, I finally punctured my notion that were I faithful or patient enough, my boyfriend would pull himself together. I was lying on an acupuncture table when

I realized it wasn't about me. These words came out of my brain and floated above me:

I can't change him.

Maybe a few more Al-Anon meetings would have gotten me there, but I like to think my liberation was ultimately conjured by pricks.

l Joined Club VIP Life

What does that even mean? I still don't know. I found it by googling "NYC matchmaking." I'm guessing the founder of Club VIP Life must have brainstormed over a bottle of pinot one night, jotted down any words that came to mind about wealthy, socially awkward older men who find spontaneous encounters to be inconvenient and threw them into a hat. Then she fished them out and assembled the words into "Club VIP Life," like entrepreneurial Magnetic Poetry. Club VIP Life is "an introduction service" that, according to the website, is also "a way of life."

Here's their mission statement:

> *Our male clients have all achieved professional success in whatever they do: physicians, attorneys, CEO's, entertainment industry professionals etc. with quality lifestyles. These men are leaders in their field looking for that special someone to share life's pleasures with.*

I was okay with the preposition hanging on for dear life at the end of the last sentence. I was less okay with the next part:

VIP LIFE attracts the most beautiful and sophisticated women interested in having a long-term relationship with dynamic and attractive men that have proven their success within the business community, and want to meet women of exceptional beauty, grace and substantive intellect.

Not only should it read "dynamic and attractive men WHO have proven their success," but the whole thing has an antediluvian smack to it. It's a matchmaking service for Men Who Work to meet Women Who Are Pretty. I was so appalled, I had to try it out. I told friends I was doing it so I could write about it, which is true. But the entire truth is that I couldn't resist seeing if I was beautiful, sophisticated, and graceful enough to join da Club. Plus, as icing on the retrograde cake, membership for the ladies is complimentary.

I submitted my online application and got a call to come in. The two women who run it were funny, smart, and down-to-earth. When I met them in person, we had a rollicking good time. I tried to appear as substantively intellectual but fun-loving as possible. I tried to look young, too. I was thirty-nine, and I figured the sun was setting on my VIP-ness in the eyes of aging "professionals etc. with quality lifestyles." I was audacious enough to tell the ladies I didn't want to meet any men over forty-nine. By the time I left, I knew I'd ducked under the velvet rope. They were already throwing names back and forth to each other about men they wanted me to meet.

We started with Julian. The way the Club works is that the men get all the info on you, the Very Important Lady-Person, including a photo. The beautiful and sophisticated women are told only the first name of the man, his general area of proven success, and maybe one other tidbit. I knew Julian was "in real estate" and had "pretty eyes." I was hopeful. Julian is a name that belongs to worldly—even foreign!—men.

Julian *was* foreign, in the way that people who are absolutely nothing like you seem to speak another language. At first I thought we might have a lot in common because we wear the same brand of jeans. I'd never met a straight man who wore Adriano Goldschmieds. I discovered the jeans thing when we spoke on the phone before our date. Make that our "meeting." It was more like an appointment he wanted me to handle. He asked where I lived and informed me my neighborhood was convenient, because he had to pick up some AG jeans nearby. Attempting a soupçon of flirtation, I asked him to pick some up for me, too. "Every man for himself," he replied, clearly a master of charm. He wanted to meet for lunch, so he could fit me into his jeans-collecting schedule.

He talked like a stoner surfer on the phone. He didn't sound like my type, but I fantasized that maybe he had a sexy Owen Wilson vibe in person. I made lunch reservations; I even curled my hair, which minimally frizzed during my two-block walk in the rain. We met.

Julian was over fifty if a day. He did have pretty, light green eyes. But let's put it this way: if Julian were Julia, he would have been bounced from Club VIP. However, I am not so very shallow that multisyllabic conversation can't overcome a superficial deficiency. And technically, according to the way this Club worked, I was the beggar and he was the chooser. After he shooed the breadbasket away without checking to see if I'd want any, I launched a tête-à-tête offensive.

ME: So, how long have you lived in New York?

JULIAN: A few years.

ME: Do you like it?

JULIAN: It's okay.

ME: Do you like to do New Yorky things—have you seen any theater?

JULIAN: I've seen a few plays . . .

ME: Oh, which ones? Anything good I should see?

JULIAN: . . . in my life. When I was a Cub Scout we had to see one, and then when I was in London I saw a play with that guy from *Friends*.

ME: Which one?

JULIAN: Ross.

Pause.

JULIAN: Oh, and I also saw that play about the French Revolution.

I spoke enough Julian by then to understand that he meant the musical *Les Miserables*. I also, at that moment, knew positively he wasn't gay. I decided to keep it simple.

ME: What do you like to do?

JULIAN: I love Glenn Beck!

ME: Oh!

Pause.

ME: Why?

Pause.

JULIAN: I don't talk politics.

Having delivered this in a tone that suggested I was try-ing to ensnare him in a debate about Middle East relations, he ushered in another round of silence.

I was like a conversation boxer staggering back to my corner, where I was filling up my spit bucket and running out of Vaseline.

Julian did not want coffee, tea, or dessert at the end of our carbohydrate-free lunch.

I took one quantum physics class in college. I didn't grasp much of it, but I seem to recall that Einstein had a theory about time slowing down. It's no theory, folks. It's true. I glanced at Julian's frozen watch every chance I could, my eyes begging its hands to move. I thought Rolexes sported second hands that swept, but Julian's second hand was like a jammed Swiffer.

The dates with other "leaders in their field" were better. No chemistry, but at least we didn't gum up the space-time continuum. My wont to interview is fairly irrepressible, so we never lacked for conversation, and by "conversation," I mean I listened attentively. And we'd say chaste good-byes, never with any utterance on their parts of "I had a great time; I'd like to see you again." I'd hear nothing and do that stupid thing where you think, *I didn't want to go out with you again, but why don't you want to go out with ME again?* Then, weeks later, I'd get a call from the Club ladies telling me that every gentleman thought we'd really hit it off and wanted more. The one exception was the lawyer doing pro bono work defending Gitmo prisoners. I'll always wonder about him. Not so much why he didn't want a second date but why someone devoted to habeas corpus petitions found himself drawn to the Club VIP Life lifestyle.

I resigned membership before I even heard of John. I didn't see it panning out, and I was a Very Impatient Person. But I got what I wanted out of it. Pathetic reassurance as I approached forty. And material, I got material.

The genetic material was to come.

I Joined Gay Date

Even my impotent attempt at using an old-school matchmaking service did not drive me to online dating. I preferred a more bespoke route to my beloved. And I found it through Gay Date.

My GBF (gay best friend), Manfred, was lunching with John's GBF, Rob, at Toast in West Hollywood. Please follow: Manfred and Rob were longtime friends, having dated in college. I knew Manfred from his grad school stint at my undergrad; I knew Rob from show biz. John knew Rob from biz, as well, and he'd met Manfred when they were both

groomsmen in Rob's wedding. Apparently, wearing match-
ing paisley yarmulkes is quite a bonding experience.

So anyway, everyone knew one another except John and
I, who both lived in Manhattan. Manfred and Rob, being
exceptional GBFs, spent their lunch bemoaning John's and
my respective relationship statuses. A giant love lightbulb
went off, and they decided to set us up. Manfred flew to New
York and took me to high tea in Gramercy Park. Manfred
is a character from another era, very Whartonian, so it was
fitting that, at a table by the garden in Lady Mendl's Tea
Salon, he described to me John's "wounded soldier eyes." His
fluency in the classics, the jaunty angle of his wedding yar-
mulke. Oh, he waxed on about this John fellow. I was sold—
oversold even. I was high on Rooibos. I was so keen that I cut
him off with my mouth full of smoked salmon finger sandwich sans crust. "Manfred, I'm in. Let's make this happen."

Introductions arrived via e-mail; John responded first
with gentlemanly alacrity, like within two hours, in a note I
read while Stairmastering.

Faith,

*Great to meet you, virtually. I should let you know that I pay
Rob and Manfred handsomely to speak well of me—I am
pleased to see they have upheld their end, and now I hope I
can live up to their billing!*

*Would be wonderful to meet in person. Please let me know
how best to be in touch. I look forward to connecting!*

Hope you're having a great day,

John S.

A hetero not afraid to use an exclamation point!! I thought. I essayed a cheeky reply:

You need a new agent: I pay those boys only AFTER any meetings to see if they really deliver. It's all about the back end, my friend. I thought you'd know this—aren't you supposed to be the business guy?

"John S." continued with his strategy of Seduction by Self-Deprecation:

Yes, I am a business guy, but I never said I was good ;-)

We agreed on a date. He suggested the place.

For Sunday, how about the Bar at the Mark Hotel?

I exercised my strategy of Seduction by Demureness:

Sure, never been, even though I've walked by it a million times on the way to my fertility doctor. I guess my mind was on other things . . . like my FSH levels.

I was testing him. If the word *fertility* were going to be a boner killer, I wanted it to slay an e-mail boner, not an in-person boner. He didn't react to this bread crumb, which I took to mean he was totally down with my FSH levels possibly being high.

I went to see an off-Broadway matinee of *The Glass Menagerie* that June afternoon and left it with high hopes about my own Gentleman Caller. I trusted the curation of Gay

Date. It also happened to be the Puerto Rican Day Parade, and I passed its detritus on the taxi ride through Central Park to the Mark as my manicure was drying. To this day I feel nostalgic when I see a drunk dude with the PR flag painted on his face.

Over three hours, I consumed two and a half glasses of wine and covered a hundred topics. Breezy, first-date ones, like both of our divorces and our dead parents and Obama. By then, I was too okay with being single to play it safe. And, by the way, did he want kids? Because I did, and soon. The wounded soldier eyes didn't flinch.

At the end of the night, I noted two novel things: John didn't care about finishing his drink, and time flew. I wasn't thinking I wanted his Ashkenazi sperm. I was thinking I wanted him to kiss me. He did.

The next morning, I thanked Manfred and Rob. Sixteen months later, they were our best men.

After we got married, Manfred and his partner, Peter, threw us a gorgeous wedding party at their Bel Air manse. They hired a shuttle service to ferry guests across the wild terrain of Beverly Glen Boulevard and up the impressive driveway. A sign on the passenger's seat at the front of the valet van read, RESERVED FOR THE ELDERLY AND PREGNANT.

I sat there, because I was both.

And when my son, Augustus, was born, I received an e-mail from Danny. It read:

JSAP = SUCCESS!!!!!!

The Final Truffle

Being deeply loved by someone gives you strength, while loving someone deeply gives you courage.

Lao Tzu

l was spread-eagle, just hanging out with my OB in her office, when we both noticed a very dark and scary mole on my inner thigh. I have a ton of moles. If that's gross, I can't help it. They're mostly flat and leave me looking like a pale Chips Ahoy cookie, but there are a couple that stick out and wobble on my midriff. My son discovered one, and after playing with it like it was a loose tooth that needed to be wiggled off, I had to take it away and distract him with a better toy, which happened to be the popener on our refrigerator. The popener is a magnet of Pope Francis that also opens beer bottles. It is arguably a choking hazard (con), but it is not attached to my body (big pro).

Anyway, there we were, Dr. Brownstein and I, seeing this mole with the fatally fuzzy boundaries that skin cancer brochures warn you about, and she said, "Faith? You really should have that looked at." *Licked* at was more like it: it turned out to be dark chocolate (65%) that smeared as soon as I touched it. This was more embarrassing than the time I discovered melted chocolate in my belly button while I was doing ab work, because no one at the gym saw me scoop that out.

I love chocolate, and when I discovered that the man with whom I was falling in love loved chocolate as much as I do, my notion of us as *beshert* was confirmed in a profound and creamy way. ("Beshert," by the way, is one of those Yiddish words that I can drop now with casual chutzpah since marrying a Jew. This new lexicon is my bounty for allowing that bloodthirsty Tribe to mutilate my son's foreskin. For a people who really need to prioritize self-perpetuation, you'd think they'd stop monkeying around down there.) And when we were first dating, John gave me a bag of truffles from Krön Chocolatier on the Upper East Side. The place is gone now, but for a time it stood like a shimmering chocolate Brigadoon with an umlaut. These truffles were exquisite: dark but not too, with the faintest aftertaste of coffee.

Just as that great American Lance Armstrong declared, "It's not about the bike," so is my story not about the chocolate. For Lance, it was really about doping and narcissism; for me, it's really about love. And saying, "I love you." Because, you see, once John gave me that bag of Krön truffles, I decided that I wouldn't finish the bag until he told me he loved me. First. *He had to say it first.*

Before I explain why John had to tell me he loved me before I would ever, EVER utter those words to him, let me clarify that this truffle thing is not a metaphor. Holding off on devouring the final truffle became a Venn diagram of Catholic self-denial overlapping superstition, with a silky center. As if I could will him to say it by wielding cacao. The bag had originally looked pretty full, a fullness commensurate with my confidence/extreme hope that I would soon hear "I love you," so I'd only jokingly promised myself I wouldn't finish the chocolate until I did hear it. But the days turned into weeks turned into months, and the truffles diminished in bites and nibbles. It wasn't a joke anymore.

I knew I was falling in love with John—perhaps I was already firmly in love with him—but I was waiting for him to announce his love for <u>me</u> in order to provide the safety net that would invite me to complete the heart's greatest bungee jump.

I can remember the moment every boy and every man told me he loved me. With Brenden, it was on a balcony of a Daytona Beach hotel during Spring Break. I was sixteen, and he held my face in his hands, and it was all I ever wanted. (Don't think for two seconds that I was allowed to go on Spring Break without my parents. My grandmother lived blocks away, and I headed back to the house where my mother grew up by 11 p.m., intoxicated but utterly sober, heart melted but perm stiffened by the sea air.) Tim L. told me he loved me as I sat behind the wheel of my red convertible while we were stopped, waiting for a train to pass. I remember the look on his face as he said it—the words tumbled out of his mouth with equal parts intensity and surprise. Jason whispered it in bed, in his Harvard dorm room overlooking the yard of Eliot House, while we were listening to *Madama Butterfly.* I recognize that the whole previous sentence reads like Mad Libs: Pretentious Edition. Andrew's British baritone purred it by the fireplace in my tiny flat above High Street in Oxford not long after I'd experienced my one and only uncircumcised willy. (Which belonged to him. It would be weird if the willy belonged to some other bloke and then Andrew said he loved me.) Trip told me while we were in his Jacuzzi, where I could envy his legs, which were much leaner than mine and glistened when he shaved them for triathlons. Then there was Tim R., who told me he loved me while he was on top of me on the purple sofa sectional in the furnished apartment I rented when I moved to New York while I was still married. Even though this filled my depleted heart, I didn't say it right back to him, because I respected the sanctity of my marriage enough not to say "I love you" immediately to my extramarital lover. And, sort of finally, after Tim Two and before Husband Two came Albert (which is not his real name since do you seriously know anyone named Albert), who told me he loved me when I was either on top of him or under him.

If you told me you loved me, and your name is missing from this list, then I am a horrible person, and I apologize, but thank you for reading this.

All those lads told me they loved me first. Which is just how I prefer it. Don't you? Learning that a man loves you—when you know you love him back and he's not creeping you out—is beyond merely flattering; it feels like an acceptance of who you are and his promise to embrace everything you want to be. Okay, sure, we know this isn't always (or even often) true: people can say they love each other but act like gaping a-holes, and a declaration of love is not always (or even often) a commitment to a future. But in that moment—that moment that can only ever happen once—when you first make yourselves totally vulnerable and create what just, against all odds, might be an eternal pact, the exchange of "I love you" feels like the most important gift. A gift that is much better received than given, if you ask me.

In writing this, I started to wonder if I wanted/needed to receive the first ILY because I am an approval junkie or if I am just a normal lady-person. So I conducted some rigorous research by e-mailing a bunch of girlfriends, a few straight guys, and one gay man. I offered them all anonymity but only had one taker, who asked to be called "Marzipan." Marzipan divulged, "I wanted him to say it first and he did. It's a holdover and old-fashioned [but] it was very important to me." Marzipan spoke for almost all the ladies who prefer that the gentleman say it first.

Only one friend said that it would probably freak her out and make her run for the hills to hear it first. But she dates people she calls "guys," preferably ones who have long hair that can be braided and swirled into a kind of hair turban. The two most mature responses both came from friends named Amy. (Coincidence? I think not. The name "Amy" means "beloved," so these women have been validated their whole damn lives, every single time someone says their name.) Here is what Beloved#1 wrote:

I will say that the phrase "I love you" is so often abused and misused and I am far less interested in its use than I am in seeing it in practice, which is usually not romantic.

And from Beloved#2:

I don't remember. I know I cared about who said it first at the time but 15 years and thousands of "I love yous" later, I just don't recall how it went down. How lame am I?

No, Amy, you are not lame. I am lame and rendered lamer by the simple loveliness of your words. And good for you for being happily married for that long to a husky Republican.*

The dudes didn't care at all who said it first, and it so happens that each of them did deliver the inaugural love address. When I asked my most voluble pal, Brad, "Did you care who said it first?" he uncharacteristically answered with the single word, "No." When I e-mailed the question to my absurdly evolved friend Jon, he pretty much wrote a poem by accident:

No—because there was nothing calculating about my wanting to say it. It was important to me to say the words, but there was no expectation in it—I just wanted her to know. My belief that this was a fact of the world that she needed to have, irrespective of what she did with it, meant that keeping it to myself wasn't an option.

And then this from Mario:

i told joe i loved him on my ex chris's ugly black pleather Ashley couch, when we were staying over at chris's place to take care of the dog.

The men's responses further comfort me that this is a gender thing. So I'll go ahead and put a tiny score for myself

---

* n.b. A year after this response, this Amy got a divorce. Even though she ended up deservedly happy, it makes me a little sad she offered such unadulterated love to that burly good ol' boy.

in the column marked "Not Totally Pathetic, Just XX." So now we can continue with my story. Because there was one man who didn't say it to me first. And his name was wasband.

I said it first. I'd waited four months and one day from our first date, but who was counting. I'd waited through a sexy New Year's Eve. I'd waited through a perfectly romantic Valentine's Day dinner. I'd waited at his hospital bedside as he came to after a minor surgery. I'd waited and waited. He came up with a catchphrase during our early days that provided a promising teaser. He'd proclaim, "I'm just swabbing the decks on Faith Salie's yacht!" Then he'd sign off phone calls with, "I miss you." So close!—just one word away! It was killing me to wait. I emotionally ruined every "important" moment by expecting it; I ruined banal moments by fervently wishing they'd become significant.

I told him I loved him on the night of my twenty-eighth birthday, right when he was walking out my door to go back to his place. I remember I was wearing a super late-'90s ensemble of pink capris and a gray-and-pink peasanty top with gray platform mules. A clip held my hair in that artfully messy *Friends*-inspired way. All in all, a late-twentieth-century appearance meant to evoke a profound declaration. For the life of me, I can remember all these details, but I can't remember why he had to go home instead of spending the night. I can picture how the sun had set and my screen door was letting in the evening breeze. I recall how it felt to tilt my head up at him and confess, softly, "I love you."

Except it wasn't a confession. It was a plea to hear it back immediately. My "I love you" really equaled "Please for the love of God tell me you love me especially because it's my birthday." It was a defunct love boomerang that never made its return journey. I must have thrown it wrong.

He didn't say it back. He didn't say, "I love you, too." He nodded like he already knew this cardiac newsflash, paused, and said ... "Thank you."

"Thank you?"

Pause.

"Is that all?"

Pause.

"I was hoping to hear you say it back."

"I know," he said. "I know how much you want me to say it. I knew how much you wanted me to say it on Valentine's Day. I know you want me to say it all the time."

"Do you not love me?" With that, of course, I started to cry.

"I'm not saying that. I just don't want to be forced to say something because you said it."

And in that moment, something occurred, which I would not understand for years to come: our dynamic was crystallized. I needed; he meted. I wanted; he waited.

So. Happy Birthday.

That was April. Obviously we continued on—I mean, this anecdote is but the juvenilia of our toxic opus. May went by, and I did a fine job of keeping my wound wide open, and we reached June. And in early June, we went to his bucolic hometown in the Finger Lakes. We were walking hand in hand at dusk at the shore of a Finger. Lightning bugs began to flicker around us—insect equivalents of Proust's madeleine for an Eastern-bred girl like me. I felt closer to him, now that his childhood was more alive to me. I also felt thin. The timing was surely right.

Crickets. Literally.

The next night we stayed at his grandfather's house. In separate bedrooms, of course, because old people think hallways are moats that prevent premarital sex. Baba, like most elderly gentlemen named Baba or Grampy or Pawpaw, was a talker, not a listener. So I listened and listened. Even before I got paid to be a professional listener, I could be an excellent listener. Of course that doesn't mean that my dark, evil mind wasn't occasionally generating judgmental commentary while my face scrunched into the "Tell me more about being a horse doctor in the '50s!" position.

Later that evening, the wasband walked in on me while I was in his grandfather's bath. Baba was not in the tub at the time. Wasband stood by the door, leaving it slightly open.

"I was watching you while you were talking to Baba. I was watching the way you listened to him, and I just want to tell you that I love you."

Pause.

My pause didn't last very long in real time. However, any pause after someone first says I love you carries weight. I knew this from recent, soul-shrinking experience. Because I possessed a generosity roughly the same size as Gollum's, I wanted to inflict upon him the weight of the wait. During that pause, a zillion feelings and thoughts passed through my heart and brain. I savored his announcement like the world's quickest but most thorough wine tasting: the immediate aroma that hit me was happiness. But happiness is such a jejune bouquet, *n'est-ce pas*? So I swirled the "I love you" around in my mental love wineglass a bit. Despite my overwhelming thirst for those three words, I summoned the resolve to make them linger there in my middle palate until they gave way to a smooth finish of resentment. Then I swallowed. His words hadn't aged better for having been bottled up. And saying "I love you" back to him didn't have the right mouthfeel.

"Thank you," I replied. Matter-of-fact; no smile, no tears. Why should I give him anything more?

I was naked. I pulled my knees to my chest.

"Will you please close the door, I'm getting cold."

I was. I was growing colder.

And that was the first time I'd felt like I possessed power in our relationship, even if it only lasted until Baba's bathroom door closed. The second time came five years later, almost to the day.

We found ourselves in Scotland. The northeast coast of Scotland to be exact, by a lighthouse, on a cliff overlooking the North Sea. The wasband pointed out that from this vantage, we stood on the very soil whence his great-grandparents hailed and looked vaguely toward his Viking ancestors. And it was there, in a spot dedicated to his patrilineage, that he asked me to marry him.

Unlike the Love Tub Episode, I totally saw the proposal coming, because, well, it was simply time. We'd talked about getting married, explicitly and erosively, for so long that it wasn't worth talking about anymore. We'd been dating for five years, which is also known as a "lustrum." But even that rococo word doesn't romanticize that half a decade is a long time to wait, and everyone in our lives was sick of it. There was an unspoken feeling of *Let's get this over with, so we can see if it will make things better.* Please buckle up, because here comes some caps lock: YES I TOTALLY KNOW THAT GETTING MARRIED IS NEVER THE WAY TO FIX

A CRAPPY RELATIONSHIP BUT I ALSO KNOW
I SHOULD FLOSS MY TEETH EVERY DAY BLAH
BLAH BLAH BLAH BLAH THANKS.

I really didn't think it would happen this one particular afternoon. This explains why I had no makeup on and had decked myself out in an Old Navy shirt, comfy jeans, and boots that supplied no flattering heel height. The wasband had gone into the Lighthouse Museum, because his great-grandfather or someone had had something to do with the building of the village lighthouse. I was exhausted (from anticipation) so I stayed in the rental car, reclined my seat, and napped. He woke me up with a knock on the window and an enthusiastic grin. "You've got to see this view!"

If you've watched *Braveheart*, you know that Scotland doesn't really give a shite that it's late May or that you're about to get proposed to, so it was wildly windy and chilly. My hair was flying everywhere. Poised on the precipice, we admired the vibrant indigo of the North Sea and the wasband's cultural provenance.

When he told me to sit on the lone bench surrounded by wildflowers, I knew. His fist was clenched, and he began to kneel. My heart started beating faster.

I shook my head. "Oh my God . . . no. Stop." *That* is what I said. Something deep inside me, beyond ego and beyond heart, knew this thing for which I'd been yearning wasn't what was best for us.

He paused midkneel, his blue-gray eyes full of hurt. Uncharacteristically, transparently, vulnerably surprised and hurt. I'd never seen that look on his face before, and I would never see it again. It lasted maybe "one Mississippi, two Mississippi," and I couldn't bear it.

"Go ahead," I said. "I'm sorry, go ahead."

He knelt down and asked me to marry him. He kept it simple. Perhaps that was a bold choice suggestive of a rebirth of our relationship, or maybe it was head-in-sandy not to acknowledge how rough our journey to this moment had been. Or, quite likely, I wasn't much of a muse after ordering him to stop proposing.

When he asked, "Will you marry me?," I looked at him through my shades, coolly. His question, like his first "I love you," created such a panoply of emotions that the best course seemed to be to try to keep my face neutral. I didn't smile or cry or gasp. I waited a few moments, my heart beating out of my chest, while I tried to relish the return of that ephemeral taste of power.

The man I deeply loved and resented, in whom I'd deeply invested, was on one knee, asking me the question I'd longed to hear since our first date. It was, in theory, the ultimate gesture of approval, but it didn't feel that way. It was too hard-earned, and that made me feel hollow. The Scottish winds carried any "power" I had out to sea. I said only, "Yes," quietly, because I wanted to. I wanted to marry him.

You don't have to believe in karma to understand this: he and I were meant to be, well, not meant to be. We had to live through the first part to realize the last part.

I couldn't wear his grandmother's ring, because it was too small. Way to feel fat at your betrothal.

We kissed and were awkwardly silent. We took a selfie on top of that cliff, years before anyone called it a selfie. In the photo, I'm kissing his cheek with my eyes closed, and he is staring right at the camera with determination. That is, neither of us is smiling in our engagement photo. I remember deciding I should kiss him, because I didn't know how genuine my smile would look if I took on the camera's eye.

We got into the car, and he asked me whom I wanted to call first. I realized I wanted to call my mom and started crying, because I couldn't afford the roaming charges to the afterlife.

Later that afternoon we stopped at Loch Ness, and my full bladder was more monstrous than Nessie. The only option was to crouch behind a rock on the shore. So I took option number only. I squatted, watching the yellow stream creep through the large pebbles, reaching my boots and then the hem of my jeans, and realized, *I'm peeing on myself on the day I got engaged*. Because that's how life can be: sometimes we pee on our storybook moments.

I'm not proud of the way I behaved that day. I took a meaningful, singular day in a youngish man's life and made certain it was not nearly as pure or joyful as he ~~deserved~~ wanted it to be. I truly hope that if and when my wasband next proposes, his words are not fraught with painful history, and the reaction he receives is not laden with hurt and entitled expectation. I also hope his future bride is big on Scots and Vikings and little of finger.

On the other hand, I forgive myself for how I reacted to his proposal. To react any other way than I did would have been transcendentally generous but disingenuous. I wasn't surprised and moved to tears. I was hurt; I was happy; I was relieved; I was confused; I was lonely; I was fearful; I was hopeful. I was human. I was honest, even though I knew my honesty hurt him. And honestly, I got a little pleasure out of hurting him—but only for that moment. The pleasure was Pyrrhic.

When my wasband didn't say "I love you" back that first time, he wanted to teach me a lesson. He wanted, foremost, to teach me that I could not coerce him into anything, even matters of the heart—especially matters of the heart. Perhaps, too, he wanted to teach me the loftier, if clichéd, lesson that really loving means giving love without expecting it in return. Or is it if you love something, set it free so that when you look down, there's only one set of footprints in the sand? All of those lessons kind of suck. Because when you give love, it feels really good to get some back. (I say "I love you" to my kids so much that they'd probably get sick of it if they were listening, but when my son <u>does</u> say, "Mommy, I love you so much" once for every forty-two times I say it to him, it's like the heavens open and drench me in pink glitter.)

But the most valuable lesson my wasband accidentally taught me, beginning that very instant he refused to say I love you, is that I wither when I withhold love. And when I say "wither" I don't mean in a beautiful, Victorian, consumptive way. I mean I shrink and get brittle. All those years I spent offering him myself and then holding myself back to tip the balance of power only succeeded in rendering myself unbalanced. Every exercise in withholding left me <u>less</u> powerful, less happy, less . . . me. When you concentrate on self-preservation, the best you can do is preserve; you don't grow. I was pickling myself. When it feels natural to express love and you <u>don't</u>, it's like stopping a gigantic sneeze over and over.

So by the time John appeared like a mensch in shining armor, I was ready to sneeze love droplets all over him. And I did—in every way but one. I never played coy; I baked for him, trekked to his apartment constantly because he was the one with dogs, scratched his chest on lazy weekend mornings, looped him in on the whole egg-freezing process I had going on, and spent kooky amounts of time in the middle of shopping at Whole Foods responding to his texts whose contents probably helped to hyperstimulate my ovaries. I even told him, when he was considering a job in LA, that I would be willing to move back there for him. What I didn't tell him was that I loved him, clearly because he hadn't told me.

I had a "relationship coach" at the time named Susan Kraker. A friend had raved about Susan, and although I was extremely wary of involving myself with anyone whose job title is "coach" but on whom I was not invited to dump a cooler of icy Gatorade no matter how victorious our partnership, I nevertheless threw my love lot in with her. I was coming off a postdivorce dating bender and craved some goal-oriented guidance. I knew John was special, and I felt a kind of urgency to make it work with him that I worried would undo our easy rhythm. I enlisted Susan to calm me down. Susan looks like the tiny love child of Janeane Garofalo and Morticia Adams. She has butt-length black hair and a sexy, crackly voice and an indefatigable interest in the romantic minutiae of her clients. She's even been known to shadow a client on a date and sit incognito at a table next to her. Susan will then pretend to read while she is really deconstructing her client's whole exchange. We'd talk on the phone for hours, and as things progressed effortlessly with John, my conversations with Coach Susan started centering around—you guessed it—The Case of the Missing "I Love You." John's behavior toward me demonstrated nothing but commitment and attraction that left me shocked I hadn't developed a UTI, so I was flummoxed by his reticence on the silly little all-important point that was consuming me. <u>Not</u> being consumed was the final truffle, sitting in my butter compartment, separated from its colleagues by my mouth and my hubris, looking less like a love token than a desiccated poopy.

Susan kept repeating something so wise that my only choice was to ignore it: she said, "You will tell him you love him when the pain of not saying it outweighs the pain of not hearing it." To which I'd exclaim, "Susan, you are not getting it! I will nevereverever say it first!!!" She knew my history. So she'd respond with something unhelpfully reasonable like, "Okay, well then, we have to come up with a strategy for waiting." As if the lone chocolate in my fridge impersonating the dropping of a medium-size rodent wasn't an effective strategy.

When he wasn't working, and I wasn't traveling for work or under anesthesia having my eggs harvested, John and I were constantly together. After only three dates, his dogs had allowed me my own side of the bed. So I knew I'd *really* miss him when, three months into our courtship, I went to Belize to do a story. And he told me that he'd miss me "terribly." When I returned, he said, he might be able to accompany me to my goddaughter's baptism at a renegade Catholic church, upstate in Rochester.

I went to the jungle for five days. Our little camp offered tons of papaya and scorpions but no cell signal or Wi-Fi. When the producer and I emerged from the heart of media darkness on our way to the airport in Belize City, I eagerly checked my phone to read John's text messages and listen to his voice mails. There weren't any. I was sad and surprised. Once I landed in New York, I could no longer take the silence. I relented and texted him, only to receive a sweet but vague response, welcoming me back and telling me he'd been spending some stressful time with his sister, who happens to be mentally handicapped. He texted me he couldn't make the baptism. I decided it was because he was dealing with family stuff and not because he was anti-Papist (this church had been excommunicated, anyway) or racist (my goddaughter is black).

I kept assuming I'd hear from him over that weekend, and I didn't. It was so unlike him that I was way more puzzled than hurt. I soldiered on, pleasantly distracted by the niceties of Spiritus Christi Church, where the priest is a woman, they never refer to God as "He," and they serve gluten-free Body of Christ. I celebrated Tallulah Gail and her daddies, David and his husband, Mark. I smiled when everyone asked how my new boyfriend was. When I got back to Manhattan, I waited to hear from John about seeing each other . . . and I didn't.

So I called Susan.

She reminded me that this was completely anomalous behavior on his part, and therefore not likely a sign that he stopped caring about me due to five days in Central America and one wafer of wheat-free Jesus. I knew she was right. And I knew I had to get answers about what was going on because—*here's the amazing part*—I wanted to make sure <u>he</u> was okay rather than primarily focus on my own disappointment.

So I told John I wanted to come over and talk to him the next day, which was a Monday. He said he was taking the day off from work, and we agreed to meet at his apartment. Now this seemed serious. Was his Talk going to be disturbingly different from my Talk?

On Monday morning, I decided to tell him I loved him. Just like that. I was sick of waiting. I loved him, I wanted him to know it, and I just plain missed him. I decided not to tell Susan I'd decided to tell John I loved him. I wanted to own the declaration completely, and I felt I'd diminish it by attending practice with my coach. Plus, I knew she'd be wildly proud of me when I sprang the news on her after the fact.

It was an un-angsty decision that made me feel strong and relieved and not sick with dread that he wouldn't say it back. With John, I didn't need to hurl a love boomerang. I was prepared to throw a one-way love Nerf dart right at his face. Before I cast myself as the Katniss of love, all dauntless and selfless, I should also say that John made me feel safe. Deep in my gut, I felt that he loved me. I thought I would probably hear him say it back . . . and if he didn't say the words, I would still feel his love and wouldn't withdraw mine.

It was a rainy, late-September afternoon. I put on some tight jeans, a striped sweater, and my Frye motorcycle boots that made me look like a fierce lesbian but always hurt when I wore them. I got to his apartment just as the dog walker was leaving with John's two dogs. Good—I could do without crotch sniffing and didn't want this conversation to be tête-à-tête-aux-furry têtes.

John looked weary. He gave me a long, tight hug. We sat on his sofa and didn't immediately have sex. I told him I was surprised I hadn't heard from him, and he apologized, launching into a list of pressures he'd been feeling from all sides, particularly regarding the needs of his sister and mother. He did not list me as one of those pressures. In fact, he told me he didn't want to drag me into his troubles. That was my cue.

"I want to be a part of your life." I surprised myself by immediately tearing up. "Because . . . I love you, John. That means that I love all of you—the easy stuff and the hard stuff. And I want you to share these things with me, and I want to help you or comfort you or just be with you. This is your life, and I want to be in it, and I want you to be in mine." Tears were rolling now—miraculously not so many that I lost my mascara if I kept my chin at just the right angle. (If you watch any *Real Housewives* reunions, you have the visual for this skill.) It felt nothing but right to tell him this and watch my words land in his big, beleaguered brown eyes.

Pause. A very bearable pause.

"I love you, too."

I inched closer to him on his sofa to hold his hand. It was quiet and rainy. It wasn't a huge dramatic or passionate moment. What it was was true, mutual, effortless, safe—all hallmarks of our relationship then and now. Okay, maybe our marriage is occasionally effortful, like when we get into it because I don't understand why John has to sneeze so loudly that I'm sure he'll wake our children and he says he can't help it and I say what would you do if you were hiding from a murderer and you had to sneeze, you would obviously stifle it, so would you please pretend there is a psychopathic killer in the house next time. Or I ask him if he will feed a child lunch and he says sure and five minutes later he is still looking at pipes on eBay and I decide that our different notions of time are keeping me from being able to *Lean* the fuck *In* so I harrumph that fine, I'll do it myself—these episodes don't always go well. Oh and also? He interrupts me all the time because he says he just wants to get to the bottom line. But mostly, like the moment we said "I love you" to each other, our relationship is gentle.

That moment was all you could ask for.

But I'm not <u>you</u>, so <u>I</u> couldn't resist pushing it. I managed to wait a little while before I had to ask him, "So, um . . . were you *thinking* you loved me? I mean, would you have said it if I didn't say it first?"

He didn't even roll his eyes. He told me he'd been thinking he loved me for a while but that words didn't matter so much to him. That other people had told him they loved him but had hurt him. That he thought the way he acted toward me made it clear that he loved me. A whole bunch of evolved answers that led me into his arms.

When the dog walker and his wards came back to find us wiping away tears, all three of them looked very confused.

I went home that evening and yanked off my too-tight boots and never wore them again. I didn't need to appear fierce or be in pain in this relationship. I stood in my socks in the kitchen and ate the final truffle. Much like the words *I love you*, it melted in my mouth.

Ovary Achiever: An Approval Junkie's Guide to Fertility

The day after my first date with the man who would become my second husband, I received a text from him.

Where are you right now?

I really liked this man. I thought he could handle the truth. I furtively clicked on my BlackBerry, which I held under the table in a conference room, "NYU Fertility Center at orientation for freezing eggs." Because there is no emoji for cryopreservation.

He wrote back, :-O

Which I took to mean, "O! you are sexily proactive!"

And so it began.

Here is a helpful guide for anyone who would also like to embark on such a tubular adventure. . . .

. . .

Decide to freeze your eggs upon suggestion of your fertility doctor. Revel in the fact that, contrary to what you'd assumed and even told Nate Berkus when you were a "practice guest" on a rehearsal for his talk show and asked him to coparent with you, you are not too ancient to do this!

Announce to everyone that you will be freezing your eggs, including the producer of an HLN pilot and your producers at *Sunday Morning*. Now both CNN and CBS cameras are lined up to film your egg retrieval. Prepare also to make gonzo, personal video diary of the freezing process.

Don't flinch when you go in for your "teach" with a nurse who shows you how to shoot yourself up in the stomach multiple times a day. Walk on air when the nurse tells you that you need a thinner needle because your abs are in good shape. Astonish yourself by actually being able to plunge a needle into your own body and decide you missed your calling as a doctor or a drug addict. Nod when nurse warns you not to exercise while hyperstimulating your ovaries, because high-impact activities could cause "ovarian torsion," which is a med-speak for "twisty tying your tubes." But tell yourself that's crazy and continue to do the elliptical and careful core work throughout this process. After all, you have camera crews following you.

Commit to a mind-body connection. Decide that you will create eighteen eggs to freeze. Eighteen because that's a lot but not too greedy, and, let's be real: reproductively, you're fairly geriatric. When you walk across Central Park every other early morning to your fertility doctor, focus on how you are investing in your future and not on all the younger women passing you with jog strollers.

Smile broadly in the darkened room as your doctor moves a wand around your ovaries and counts and measures your follicles. Thank her when she announces you have "amazing ovaries." Try to be humble about it (*"Oh, these old things?"*), but secretly wonder if you are manifesting all this with the mind-body connection you are cultivating. Call your father and brothers to report on your high numbers as you walk back through Central Park toward the non-high-impact exercise you will do at the gym.

See this new man John as much as possible. Wonder if all this chemistry between you is helping your eggs swell. Time your dates around injections. Keep him posted, hoping that this whole process will make you appear as someone who is goal oriented but doesn't have to get pregnant tomorrow or even the next day, but the day after that would be okay. Leave some cookie dough you've made for him in his freezer to distract from the drugs you've left in his refrigerator. When he offers to take you to the egg retrieval, kindly decline and say you're covered, so as to have an air of mystery about you.

Be sure to work out extremely early in the morning before egg harvest so you look thin on camera—in a hospital gown, underneath the sheets—because you are a freak. Put on makeup. Greet CNN and CBS camera crews at entrance to NYU Fertility Center. Go in, go under, come out. Learn that you produced twenty-one eggs, exactly eighteen of which are worthy of being frozen, *which is eggsactly the number you wanted.*

Your friend Elliot, son of a rabbi, teaches you that, in

Judaism, the number eighteen is sacred. It is "chai." Not
the Oprah kind that Starbucks sells, the kind that is pronounced as if you're trying to expel a hairball.

It means "life."

High-five yourself on mind-body connection.

Explain to your boyfriend that there's just really no way you
can get pregnant naturally, you never have; it would be a
miracle. Begin using no contraception whatsoever. Do not
convene A Talk About Having a Baby Together. Everything's been pretty effortless so far, and although you and
your boyfriend have not technically decided to get married,
because you've only been dating for four months, implicitly
understand that you are each other's Second Chance, and
you'd like to create a family together. Find improbability of
conception confirmed about every forty days—dramatically
so on romantic trip to Marrakesh where you learn that Mus-
lims aren't big on tampons, so you just make do with some
toilet paper, which they're not real big on either.

Eleven months after your first date, when your breasts start
feeling like fiery tennis balls, take a pregnancy test for kicks.
When you notice that the pregnancy test says "PREG-
NANT" for the first time in your forty years, say, out loud,
"Oh my God." Go to CVS in your PJs and buy five more,
daring them to say the same thing. Call your brother. Tell
him the amazing news while he almost crashes his car into a
support structure in the State Department parking garage.
Wait all day to tell your boyfriend in person. Expecting an

overjoyed response, try not to be disappointed when he acts just joyed and smiles serenely and says, "Why not?" Recognize that this man of yours, he has a profound belief in good things happening.

Tell almost everyone, because you want to demonstrate that you do not believe in jinxing. Do the math and realize you were actually pregnant when your boyfriend took you to look at engagement rings on Mother's Day, historically your least favorite day of the year. Intuit it's a girl. Name her Sursie, which is a southern word for "surprise gift."

Google image "empire-waist wedding dresses" for at least forty-five minutes a day.

When you are seven weeks along, watch nothing move on the ultrasound. Try to be stoic. Try not to be the hysterical woman in the fertility office whom you're sure your doctor has seen a thousand times. Do not sob until you walk out of her office and your boyfriend can hold you on the corner of Madison and Seventy-Seventh. Go to the Mark Hotel across the street where you had your first date and drink some tea, which you can now sweeten with as much Sweet'N Low as you choose. You can even stir some Brie in there if you'd like. Don't say too much but hold hands a lot. When your boyfriend walks you home through Central Park, call your father. When you hear him cry, your heart breaks all over again.

Host a live comedy show that night, even though all you want to do is to curl up in a fetal position. While you are in the green room, accept an offer from BBC America to fly to London to shoot a pilot with Graham Norton. This does not take away the pain, but note that really sad things and pretty cool things can happen in tandem.

On your way home from London, begin bleeding in the Virgin Upper Class Lounge. Try to distract yourself by watching Meryl Streep on one side of the lounge and David Hasselhoff on the other. On the flight home, sit one row directly behind a very handsome man and his wife and their nanny and their toddler son and baby daughter. When the man says to you "I'm sorry" about the ruckus his kids make, use everything you have not to tell him that his noisy life is your dream and that you're going to the bathroom several times an hour because you've lost your first baby.

When you return, have a D&C in your fertility doctor's office without anesthesia, because it appears that the "spontaneous abortion" is almost complete. Still, it hurts like hell, but you are strong; you can do this. Accept the frosted sugar cookie the nurse gives you after the procedure to help your blood sugar. Or to cheer you up. It is a purple-and-yellow flower. Actually eat the entire sugar cookie, which is something you'd never otherwise do.

When you get engaged ten days later in front of the Fountain of Four Rivers in Piazza Navona, appreciate that you have exactly forty-five minutes before your first appointment to look at wedding venues. Yes, you knew you were going to get engaged on this trip, so good thing you're wearing the floral "engagement dress" you purchased just for this moment! Which, excuse you/me, is in no way presumptuous, since you both decided to go to Rome to choose a place to get married, even though he hadn't asked you yet. You're no longer premaritally pregnant, but he's still going to make an honest woman out of you. You two are old-fashioned like that.

. . .

Decide that a round of IVF is just the thing a bride needs
to distract her from planning a foreign wedding in three
months as well as finding a new place to live with her fiancé
that will accept his two smelly dogs. Listen to fiancé suggest perhaps this is a lot to take on? Assure him it is not, as
forward motion is healing, and every month matters to you.
You will save frozen eggs for making baby number 2 when
you are even older. Impress nurse at your refresher teach
with how unsqueamish you are about giving yourself the
shots. Fire up mind-body connection. Go through the whole
injection process again, but this time with specific sperm in
mind. As the process unfurls, try not to blame yourself that
your follicles aren't as prodigal as they were last time. When
your fertility doctor calls an audible and advises punting by
turning this into an artificial insemination, say sure. Having
intrauterine insemination (IUI) allows you to pretend you
are one-half of a celebrity lesbian couple.

Explain to your fiancé how he needs to produce a "sample" that will be brought with swiftness to your doctor's office. Present yourself as the world's most perfect partner by
offering to help him produce this sample the old-fashioned
way rather than having him take things into his own hands.
As soon as you, Team IUI, produce sample together, leap
off him and nestle cup o' sperm in your tiny cleavage inside your running bra to keep it at optimal temperature.
Give him a kiss and racewalk from Second Avenue across
Park Avenue, being careful not to slosh the genetic material. When you bump into an acquaintance en route, feel
lucky that you do not literally bump into him and endeavor

to be friendly but not engaging enough to allow for deleterious cooling of semen. Do not mention you're holding a wad between your boobs.

Upon learning that your fiancé's usable sperm count is solidly in the millions with excellent motility, feel proud that you have chosen such a potent spouse and wonder if your whole mind-body connection thing is infectious. Lie back, relax, and let millions of sperm swim toward five good eggs. Visualize their doing so. Resolve that, with those odds, there's no way you won't get pregnant. When the doctor tells you that you can leave, go the extra mile by reclining longer while texting your fiancé the good news about his sperm count. In fact, text your whole family so that your father calls him "33 Mill" for a while, as if his future son-in-law is a rapper.

When at-home pregnancy tests reveal that you are not, in fact, pregnant, try not to take it too hard. When blood tests at the doctor's say you were pregnant for two seconds, try to put a positive spin on it, as if two seconds is better than no seconds. Do not grieve this "chemical pregnancy" as a second miscarriage, because that seems way too pro-life. Convince yourself that the upside is you can now attempt to get drastically thin for your fast-approaching wedding. Being thinner for your second wedding than your first seems like an admirable goal.

So as not to be a slacker, put another round of IVF on the calendar for the week after your honeymoon. Get preliminary blood work done two weeks before your wedding. While at the CBS offices, working on one of your stories for *Sunday Morning*, return a call from nurse about your blood test. Be shocked when she tells you you are pregnant, naturally. So shocked that you step out of the building, onto West Fifty-Seventh Street, where you explain to her that she is mistaken. She explains that *you* are mistaken, and you are indeed pregnant. Call your fiancé and announce the good news/bad news in one breath, as taxis rush by and the revolving door spins behind you: "Okay are you ready for this I'm pregnant but let's not make it a big deal because it's not going to last."

Do a little math and accept the fact that you got pregnant with the aid of the Eternal City and not science on a last-minute wedding planning trip on September eleventh. Gloat that the terrorists didn't win. Nevertheless, assume that you will have a miscarriage during your wedding weekend or honeymoon, which is highly annoying. Have this pessimism more gently confirmed by your fertility doctor, who gives you about a 20 percent chance of this pregnancy lasting. But just in case this thing is going to happen, stop starving yourself. Put down the Sprite Zero and back away. Eat mostly hard-boiled eggs until you leave for Rome.

Tell very few people you are pregnant. When you feel intense pain a few nights before your wedding, wait for the blood to come. Observe, with surprise, that it never does. Discover it makes your wedding more intimate and romantic that you and your new husband are creating a new life together in more ways than one.

The day before you get married, take a nap with your man. While you lie there, talk to the life inside you, if, in fact there's still life inside you. Thank it for being there, for however long it's with you. Then drink a touch of Prosecco and Frascati and dance gymnastically like a dirty whore with your gay brother at your wedding reception. Feel like what is meant to be will be, and this day is for celebration, and this teensy soul is celebrating with you.

On your honeymoon, notice that you feel really sick while walking to see David—the statue, not your brother, whom you did not invite on your honeymoon. Sit down on a bench on the streets of Florence. Realize, with insane gratitude, (a) this is what pregnancy nausea feels like! and (b) I need a nap!! Attend vespers all over Florence and Venice to light candles for your baby. Dare to hope.

Two days after returning from your honeymoon, go to the doctor with your husband. Witness a heartbeat on the ultrasound. Watch tears roll down his face while you smile so hard your cheeks hurt. Text your family and your friends April and Joanne: "Heartbeat!!!" In celebration, hold hands and walk to a café where you split a smoked salmon on pumpernickel sandwich because you know about the no sushi but you don't know yet about the no smoked salmon.

Have a complicated pregnancy of Advanced Maternal Age. Take good care of yourself, because this little guy needs you to.

Become a mother at forty-one.

Celebrate your first real Mother's Day on national television. Perform a CBS commentary about being a new mother in [gulp] middle age. Talk about how you have some gray in your roots, but your baby doesn't care because he can't see the top of your head, and how you probably need glasses at your age, but you keep your son close so you don't have to squint to see him. Try not to cry as you deliver these words. Cry a little when you receive beautiful, grateful responses from viewers. Smile a little at the man who comments that it's selfish to have kids at your age. And the other guy who blames feminism.

Tick tock: when your son is four months old, see your fertility doctor about getting pregnant again. Time to get your money's worth from those frozen eggs. Make a plan for starting meds and shots, pump breast milk for your son right up until you have to go on hormones to try to be Best Mother Ever. When your seven-month-old son awakens ridiculously early in the mornings, go running with him in jog stroller so your husband can sleep. Return at 8 a.m. on the dot with cranky baby to have well-rested husband inject your upper ass quadrants with progesterone. Apply lavender-scented, microwavable teddy bear to your butt ASAP. Shove into running pants and walk around with hot bear butt while you chase the baby.

Pee on sticks at 3 a.m. because you can't wait for blood test. Tell your platonic soul mate, Joanne, you are pregnant before anyone else. Prepare for your husband to take the news in stride. "Why not?" he says again. Don't bother to explain that "Why not?" could be that you've lost one and a half pregnancies, and you're almost forty-two, and the odds of IVF working are less than 30 percent. Try to invest in his sanguinity. Mind-body connection blah blah blah.

Feel really sick. Love it. Embrace it. When you actually vomit—the only time you've ever thrown up while pregnant—in front of your concerned baby boy, celebrate. Do math: vomiting + heart beating on multiple ultrasounds =

baby! Secretly hope it's a girl. Go away from your son for four days to host a TV show and be a panelist on *Wait Wait . . . Don't Tell Me*. Dare to confide in copanelist and great guy Bobcat Goldthwait you are pregnant after you two reminisce about being on the same '90s sitcom that also starred a stuffed bunny named Mr. Floppy. Justify being away from an eight-month-old baby for almost a week by telling yourself you're spending time with your other child. Lie in bed at the Hyatt and put your hand on your belly and thank the new baby.

On an offensively frigid day in March, see no heartbeat on the ultrasound. You can't see the monitor, but you can see your OB looking at the monitor. Know something is very, very wrong when she narrows her eyes and tries not to frown. Squeeze your husband's hand but not as tightly as you squeeze your eyes shut. Silent tears escape anyway and roll down your cheeks. When your husband wants to connect with you and hold you, all you can do is contract into stasis, much like your baby who has recently died. Try not to wonder when—at what moment—its heart stopped beating. Try not to think of it just floating inside you, lifeless.

Stay silent when your doctor sends you to the hospital to have the miscarriage confirmed on a larger screen by a more powerful instrument. Remind yourself, as you walk through the burn unit, there are worse things than a miscarriage.

When your husband leans in to cry together face-to-face as you lie on the gurney, push him away so you can see the screen. Explain, "I have to see. I have to see the baby." You need to witness the heart not beating. You owe that to this child—to look. It's an open casket and your way of saying good-bye.

Resolve not to be so judgmental about pro-lifers, except for the ones who blow up doctors.

Stop crying when your husband needs to cry, and put your arms around him. Take turns. Take a cab home.

As soon as you walk in the apartment, find your little guy. He is wearing his PJs with the monkey on the butt. Sing to him and put him in his crib. Notice that you cannot cry when you are holding your healthy baby and watching him fall asleep by propping his monkey butt in the air. *Be grateful, be grateful, be grateful. You have more than some people ever have.*

Drink the half glass of Priorat your husband gives you and informs you is a fine glass of wine. Take a hot bath, sniffle. Put away the pregnancy books by your bed and take out Dickens's *Our Mutual Friend*. But before you climb into bed, do something that you haven't done in a long, long time: tiptoe into your son's dark room and lay your hand on his chest.

You need to feel his heart beat.

After your D&C (this one in the hospital with anesthesia), bleed for weeks and weeks. Stay sad for a long time. Learn that your uterus is made of Velcro and has clung to what is medically termed "POC," or "products of conception." Upon learning this, forgive yourself for being so sad, because now you understand that your body was cleaving to this lost baby, so it makes sense your heart was, too. Have another surgery to yank the POC off your Velcruterus.

When you learn that there was no chromosomal reason for the miscarriage, and that the pro-choice fetus/pro-life baby was a boy, irrationally blame yourself. Feel certain that this little XY spirit knew you wanted a girl and so departed. Feel awful. Ask your fertility doctor what you can do to prepare for next time—you have nine eggs left. There must be something you can do, to do this better. She tells you to use these weeks to heal and enjoy your family before you will, once again, be beholden to timed injections, blood tests, and a hot teddy bear in your pants.

You have not been able to travel for a long time because of the fertility treatments, so tag along on your husband's business trip to Paris. Encourage your son to smear fancy Opéra cake all over his face on his first birthday. Light candles at Notre Dame. Go to Rome and rub St. Peter's foot at the Vatican for good hormone levels.

A couple months later, start all over again. Feel proud of the one egg you choose to put in, because NYU Fertility Center has given it an "A." Wish you could do extra credit to make it an "A+." Save the photo of the day five blastocyst, which looks a bit like a moon crater or a pizza or a condom but may turn out to look like you. Put your son in the baby carrier and walk with him to Blessed Sacrament every morning, where you lean over and allow him to grab unlit candles. Pay for candles so you don't go to hell. Light them. When you kneel down to pray to Mary, because she's a woman and probably gets it even if she definitely did not do fertility treatments, feel with satisfaction that this is a really good glutes, hams, and quads work out, since you are carrying twenty pounds of viable child. Smile back at the homeless woman wearing a turban who's always sitting or snoozing in the back pew. And when your Jewish husband occasionally joins you in these prayers, thank G-d that you married him, because you remember how, on your first honeymoon, your Episcopalian wasband refused to visit famous French cathedrals, disgusted as he was by the history of the Catholic Church.

Promise yourself you will not take a pregnancy test too early. Ignore your promise immediately and tinkle as quietly as possible on a stick at blur-thirty in the morning. Feel your heart swell as two lines emerge. Refrain from waggling the pee stick in front of your sleeping husband's face and screaming joyously, "WHY NOT?!!" Pee on more sticks for days, because the lines keep getting darker and more beautiful. Save the sticks in the cabinet by your nail polish like a fertility hoarder.

Promise God that you would love a little brother for your son. Name him Rufus to prove you're serious. "Rufus," which is Latin for "red," because you hope he will have fake red hair like you.

Tell no one about this pregnancy except Joanne and John. Even put water in your Sprite Zero bottles to drink during the Sirius radio show you host so that your cohost has no clue, because you once told her that if you ever stopped drinking diet soda, she'd know you're pregnant.

When you're ten weeks pregnant, and you discover you're having a girl, try hard to believe it. Try not to mind that the first person you tell is the nanny you will later fire for stealing from you, because she's right there when you hang up the phone. Go to Rome for your anniversary, and when you are walking through Piazza della Minerva, remember that this is the first place you ever stayed with your now-husband, at the Grand Hotel de la Minerve. Recall strolling by the square's Bernini elephant statue with your mother almost twenty years before. Walk with your son and husband into Santa Maria sopra Minerva, the basilica with the cobalt blue ceiling painted with stars, and light candles once more for your son's sister. Decide you will name her Minerva. Note that you light a ton of candles. Hope the proceeds are not going toward the care and feeding of old pedophiles.

Think it's a good idea to give birth this time without any drugs, so you can see what your body can do. At forty-two weeks, receive a saffron bath as your water breaks. Experience the walloping physical agony to which you psychotically committed. Drip amniotic fluid on Carlos the doorman's shoes as you shuffle into a taxi. Promise taxi driver you will not give birth in his vehicle. Vomit in the lobby of Labor & Delivery as you moan, "GOD HELP ME." When you tell them you have to push, and they tell you to wait, listen to your body and push. When they whisk your daughter away as she leaves you and enters the world, covered in meconium, feel like your heart is across the room wailing to be returned to your body.

A few months later, return to Blessed Sacrament to light a candle (of course) on what would be your mother's seventieth birthday. Cherish the fact that your prayers are now "Thank you" rather than "Please." Wonder why God has given you so much. Thank your children for choosing you. Thank the babies who were yours for weeks for paving the way for the babies who are now yours for life. Also observe that this kneeling involves only thirteen pounds of new baby, so genuflect a few extra times to target postpartum glutes. Notice the turbaned homeless woman. Smile. Wonder if she realizes that you're the same lady who prayed and prayed for the little girl in the pink floral sun hat whom you're now carrying in front of your heart.

Wait Wait ... Don't Tell Me About Batman's Nipples

When your joke sucks, there's no difference between performing in front of fifteen thousand people or five hundred people. The silence produced by a large crowd not laughing sounds exactly the same as that of a more intimate audience. I discovered this not too long ago during a *Wait Wait ... Don't Tell Me!* taping in Chicago's Millennium Park, in front of a sea of the show's fans.

If you're not a fan of the show, you should be, for reasons having nothing to do with me. Like most panelists, I appear on it about once a month. But the program has almost five million weekly listeners, and it's been on air—and now podcasting—for almost twenty years, so it's doing something very right. *Wait Wait ... Don't Tell Me!* (or WWDTM, as we acronym-hungry NPR types write) is a quiz show in which a regular rotating cast of comedians and writers makes jokes about the week's news. It tapes on Thursdays in front of a studio audience and then gets edited and aired over the weekend. Its host is Peter Sagal, a public radio rock star who makes sardonic sexy, and his sidekick/scorekeeper was, for sixteen years, the iconic Carl Kasell, the most avuncular gentleman in radio. Now Peter's joined by self-proclaimed "legendary anchorman" Bill Kurtis, a playful *éminence grise* with a voice groovy enough to make Ron Burgundy drop an egg.

The public radio tribe is a fairly small clan of resiliently nerdy folks. Even after my own show was canceled, I remained family. I asked my agent to reach out to WWDTM, and the producers took a chance on me. They invited me to be on a show, and I figured if I didn't screw up, I might get asked back. So this would be an audition, really, that millions of people would get to hear. I felt like I was from New Jersey and being invited to jam with The Boss. I wanted to crush it.

A couple of days before I flew to my first taping in Chicago, Peter called to give me some tips. I tried, as I walked through Central Park with the phone to my ear, to get used to hearing the voice that had become so familiar through my radio, talking to *me*, just me, so warmly. Peter said he knew I might feel nervous (yes) but not to be (ha) and then offered two main pieces of advice. He suggested I say whatever jokes popped into my head before figuring out whether they're funny. "Half the stuff gets edited anyway, for time," he said. "We'll protect you from sounding like an idiot." He continued, "And if something calls to mind a personal story—it doesn't have to be funny, just true—give it a shot. You never know where things may lead."

Peter's advice indeed proved helpful. At my debut,

beloved panelist Mo Rocca, who happens to be a college friend, put me at ease as soon as the catchy WWDTM theme song started. Sitting in front of our mics at the panelist table, he started swaying his shoulders to the music. Then he began shimmying like he meant it, and I could not help but choose to join him. We looked like a pair of Muppets. That was my first taste of how much more fun this radio show was in person. I did fine that first time, won a few laughs, got asked back. And asked back again. It took me a couple of years, though, to stop worrying about whether I was offering enough funny to become a regular.

I also had to embrace the fact that being part of the show means getting laughs that most people will never hear. We record for close to two hours, but the final version that airs is less than an hour; stuff gets cut. This happened with that Millennium Park show, after a caller named Connie informed us she was an OB-GYN. She was playing "Bluff the Listener." Bluff the Listener asks the contestant to hear three ridiculous stories based on a common topic, one of which is actually true. The producers e-mail us the night before and assign one of us to write up the real story and the other two panelists to concoct fake ones. (I type mine on the plane to Chicago so I can refine it all day; Mo, in contrast, often scratches out something priceless—perhaps even with an obscure early '80s TV reference, like Gavin Mac-Cleod—in the green room just before we take the stage.) During this particular show, with Dr. Connie, I had the real story, and she didn't choose it, which would have won me a point in the game. Instead, she dithered between the other fake stories written by my two male colleagues, so I rebuked her. "Connie," I said, "you should stick with vaginas." For better or for worse, it was my biggest laugh of the night, which you missed if you listened to that show. They edited it out. I guess because it's public radio, not *pubic* radio.

For a while, I tried to figure out my role on the show. I don't bring the bold comedy chops of panelists Paula Poundstone and Alonzo Bodden, who tour the country doing stand-up. I don't have the inspired irascibility of veterans like Charlie Pierce and Roy Blount Jr. I find a comfort zone being a bit of the wonky one, not a know-it-all—because I don't know it all, at all—but the one who's done enough research to add a bit of trivia to the news stories. Also, I'm usually the only woman onstage when I do a show,* and I've discovered that being transparent about my unique perspective often pays off. I've learned to trust myself to be more funny than clever. An audience can usually sniff out prefab jokes, and if they can't, my fellow comedians nail me on it: "You've been sitting on that one, haven't you, Faith?" Jokes are not made to sit on. Neither are these lessons I've learned over my years on the show.

Make Your Notes Disappear

I study for this show like Tracy Flick on Adderall. I spend the day of the taping in the hotel room, tirelessly clicking from one news site to another, checking constantly for updates (Drudge and FARK are my best friends on those days). On a legal pad, I scrawl headline after headline:

---

* The producers rarely put two ladies on the same panel, the exception being Paula, who often gets to perform with another woman, because her comedy apparently possesses an androgynous quality.

"Man shoots armadillo; bullet hits mother-in-law," "Linguists say Trump talks like 3rd grader." It's my pregame ritual. The other comedians mock me for this. Sometimes Adam Felber leans over onstage and pretends he's cheating by trying to decipher my cursive. But they're not cheat sheets. I just feel more confident with pages in front of me, because their very presence reminds me that I've done all the homework I can do, and now it's time to stop kneeling to the Geeky Preparation Gods and start invoking the Impromptu Comedy Gods. And anyway, one of the hallmarks of WWDTM is questions you could never possibly answer, like, "Prime Minister David Cameron has vowed never to do what?" (Answer: "Point at fish.")

I always think, when I glance down at my copious notes, if my jokes don't kill tonight, at least I can win the news questions in the winner-determining Lightning Round. Even in my early middle age, I still, pathetically, want to ace the test. Plus, my stage-father sends me a no-pressure text before every show: "Please do honor to the family name."

I learn more, however, from studying the signature ways of my colleagues than from refreshing the Drudge Report. There's the intellectual wackiness of Luke Burbank that charitably assumes the audience will catch his esoteric references. There's the self-effacing charm of Tom Bodett, which teaches you can actually be a pleasant person <u>and</u> a comedian. Adam is the Generous Gentleman of Comedy, probably because he's a successful television writer who's made a career out of making others sound funny. He never steps on your joke and cheerfully invites you to take his and pun-run with it. When Mo answers a question, he sounds like he's playing an urgent game of Password. He has no fear that voicing his stream of consciousness will embarrass him. I've borrowed this from him—a faith that thinking out loud might be funny. Try it—it's a bit scary to do in front of one person, much less millions. However, I can never borrow from the unfiltered rants of Paula. They are inimitable. Even if she's not exactly saying something funny, her indignation at the way the world works makes her a comic genius.

Some trios have better chemistry than others, and you leave the show feeling like everyone played a great game, because you tagged one another's jokes in a kind of comedaraderie, which is a word I just made up and kind of like. We all hope to push away from the table after recording, feeling like it was that kind of show. It doesn't always happen. Even Peter, who has unfailingly delivered laughs for going on twenty years, very occasionally remarks, after leaving the stage, that he wishes a show had felt funnier.

While writing this chapter, I reached out to my fellow panelists to ask them how they prepare. The first person to e-mail me back was Charlie Pierce, who never tires of mocking/celebrating the ancient Roman roots of my children's names.

You mean other than using my Jesuit training in the classics to think up cool names for your kids??
How are Hadrian and Calpurnia?

The second to respond was my pal Adam Felber.

17 years ago, when the show was in its infancy, I hardly prepared at all. Even if I knew an answer, I often went for a joke instead. Who cares? I thought. I'm FUNNY. Then

one day, one of the producers called me. Anyway, he confirmed that I was funny (yay!) . . . and then let me know that if I wanted to stick around on the show, I needed to win every once in a while. I literally couldn't have afforded to lose the gig at that point, so I hit the books.

Since that day, I've pretty much had the same method: The Wednesday before the show I'll hit one news site (it changes, but always one of the big services), and read the past week's worth of world, national, political, and entertainment headlines. Then I'll hit a site or two that aggregates weird or funny stories and do the same.

After that reading, I'm done. I don't try to come up with a take on the news or arm myself with quips. I think of my long years doing improv as my comedic Cialis: When the time comes, I'll be ready.

Two of the women panelists chimed in.
From Kyrie O'Connor:

I decided early in life, long before I knew what a feminist was, that I was not going to be the Girl Who Studied. Nobody liked that girl unless they needed to copy her homework. My strategy of trying to absorb enough from the universe to get by worked well in high school, badly in college, and aces in the workplace where, let's face it, nobody's all that bright. For "Wait Wait," I figured out early on that if I checked npr.org for what regime was overthrown and fark.com to see who stuffed frozen king crab down his pants, I'd be OK.

And from Amy Dickinson, of "Ask Amy" fame:

I channel my favorite person from my childhood TV watching, Rose Marie, from *The Dick Van Dyke Show*. I simply try to do what I think she would do. Would Rose Marie wear a dress? Spray her hair with Aqua Net? Yes, yes, she would. Would she try to wisecrack her way past Dick Van Dyke, Morey Amsterdam, and Carl Reiner? Yes—she definitely would.

I try to read the newspaper regularly the week I'm on the show, but mainly I am never very prepared—everything I think I know flies out of my head backstage and I'm trapped with only the outfit and helmet hair as protection. When I don't know the answer to a question, which is almost always, I try to set myself on fire so at least as I go down—I'll go down in flames. The men I tend to be booked with on the show don't seem to prepare at all. They don't even really bother to get dressed.

Then this from Maz Jobrani, who doesn't mind being known as "the Persian Pink Panther":

When I first started I would read CNN.com the week of the show and also go on Fark.com. Now since I've got two young kids and have a pretty busy work schedule, I find myself cramming the day of. I also try to listen to NPR whenever I'm in the car, but my four-year-old daughter keeps wanting to hear Nick Jonas so that doesn't help! Unless there's a question about Nick Jonas, in which case I'll probably get that one right. (By the way, as a comedian I had an epiphany that my job isn't to win the show but to try to be funny. Seems like whenever I win I'm less funny. Hmmm.)

And from Alonzo Bodden, who won *Last Comic Standing*:

I might have a chance to look at the NPR app and see what's trending but usually I show up knowing there'll be at least one question that I will know nothing about. They ask me about a naked guy shopping in a German grocery store, then they ask Maz, the Iranian, about Iran. It's just not fair.

I'm not sure how others prepare but I just have a good time and stay funny in the moment, and, oh, I try not to do shows with Adam. He's pretty sharp.

Please read this, from Roy Blount Jr, in his southern accent, which places you in a rocking chair on a porch in south Georgia.

I immerse myself in fark.com, which keeps me at the cutting edge of weird news developments, for as long as I can stand it—about an hour and a half on Tuesday. Then I cry out, "Enough!" and plop my fate onto the laps of the gods, preferably Venus's but she's so crowded.

P. J. O'Rourke sent the following, which I'm certain he composed in between cigar puffs:

Prepare? What is this meaning "prepare?" We do not have this in my country.

I've got a five-page list of things to do/buy/sort/pack before I leave on even a one-day hunting trip—beginning with American Kennel Association registration papers for dog's dame and sire and ending with whiskey, 5 gallons. I have a one-sentence memo to myself about doing WWDTM: "Read Thursday's *New York Times*." And I usually don't make it through that, getting stuck in the obits, trying to remember if I knew that guy back in the 1960s.

I've been a reporter for 45 years. By now, there's no such thing as "that's news to me." Just the names change. And since I can barely remember my own, what's the use?

I do, however, work hard on my Bluff, making sure it rings at least a tiny bell of believability and has a punch line. Then I carefully do not e-mail it to WWDTM ahead of time, to keep [Executive Producer Mike] Danforth from pissing in it.

From Tom Bodett:

I have an hour-and-a-half drive to the airport and listen to the XM radio feed of headline news with Robin—the talking head—Meade. It is excruciating. She comes across as a chatty neighbor who reads the front page of your newspaper on her way across the lawn and is now filling you in—but the pain helps me think.

I buy a *NY Times, NY Post, USA Today* and a bag of peanut M&Ms for the flight. When I get to the hotel in Chicago, or wherever, I rewrite the bluff then spend an hour looking at weird news online—the exploding toilets and llamas in the trunk of a Florida couple's car, which are the bread and butter of WWDTM—that are not covered, even by Robin Meade. One must dig deeper.

Once I'm suitably informed I take a nap and wake up refreshed to find I've forgotten almost everything I learned that day. I walk to the theater, eat the free food, and try to distract the other panelists from their work with pictures and stories of my children and pets.

And, at last, a real answer from Charlie arrived.

Because what I do for a living immerses me in Da Big stories of the day for about eight hours out of every 24, I don't need much show prep on them. But I do check back a week on Fark, because that's where you find the stories about humans smuggling ferrets in their pants and about stupid criminals. Both of these are guaranteed winners in the later questions of the lightning round.

I must have my 3–5 nap before every show or I get cranky.

Give my best to Diocletian and Livia.

Reading my comrades' answers confirmed for me my hyperactivity when it comes to homework and taught me three important things: (1) Fark is not the secret weapon I thought it was, (2) when I'm an older man, I can take a nap before the show, and (3) spontaneity trumps preparation.

If you listen to the show, you know the best bits are completely spontaneous. One of my favorite moments came when I was just plain honest. Peter explained that when researchers had asked couples to have more sex, the couples who complied by getting it on reported themselves as getting less happy. This floored me.

FAITH: What??

ADAM: Well, of course.

PETER: I know.

FAITH: What do you mean, of course?

ADAM: Well, you think that just forcing a couple to have twice as much sex is going to make them happier?

FAITH: If someone forced me to have sex, it would be really good . . . [*all of a sudden realizing how horrible this sounds in every possible way*] I mean consensually! . . . And with my husband!!

PETER: Don't call in, America.

BOBCAT GOLDTHWAIT: If somebody forced you to have sex with your husband? That's the weirdest statement ever. How did you even get kids?

I can't study for an exchange like that. I definitely did not craft any jokes there, because I wasn't joking. And maybe it's for the best that my husband rarely listens to the podcast.

Make an Assist

Approaching the War Memorial Opera house in San Francisco—at 3,146 seats, the largest venue in which I'd ever performed, until the Millennium Park show—I experienced one of those, "Wow, take it all in" moments. Like I'd arrived.

Until I arrived at the door next to the box office. A woman was picking up her *Wait Wait . . . Don't Tell Me!* tickets.

"Who's doing the show tonight?" she asked the Box Office Person.

[Muffled Charlie Brown's teacher sounds from Box Office Person]

"Who? Faith Salie??" lamented the lady. "But we wanted Paula!"

It's not big fun to be reminded that you're not someone's favorite. I get why fans love Paula. Besides the bright red lipstick she always applies just before we go onstage, I have no idea whether she prepares for the show—she doesn't need to, since her kind of humor transcends topical jokes.

I've found over the years that one of my functions on the show is to cue up someone else's comedy, even inadvertently. I'm not always the funniest, and I've grown comfortable with that. Because a show that makes the audience laugh is a great show whether or not *I* made them laugh. Here's an exchange with one guest named Brenda who introduced herself as a literary agent for children's books:

FAITH: Brenda, I have a question about children's books?

BRENDA: Yes.

FAITH: With all due respect, I sometimes feel about them the way I do about modern art, where you look at it and you go, "I could do that."

BRENDA: I bet you do, Faith. And maybe you would like to write a children's book.

FAITH: I got one about a monkey afraid of the dark.

PETER: I don't think you respect the form, Faith. That's what I think.

PAULA: I remember once I was cleaning up late at night, I was putting things away. And I came across a book, I don't know who bought it, but it was a cardboard book called *The Book of Shapes*. And I swear to you, it was six pages long, and that's because it went as far as oval. And I looked at the cover, and it was coauthored. By the way, the books that have sponges in them . . . that go in the bathtub? The text isn't any good at all.

Paula took my premise and sprinted with it. Farther and faster than I could, and she was hilarious. Sometimes you make an assist, and the whole team wins. Sometimes you're John Stockton to someone else's Karl Malone.

I had to ask my husband for that sports metaphor.

Make a Mistake

Perhaps the best part of doing WWDTM is the freedom to say stupid shit. Sometimes you say stupid shit on purpose, because it's a lame joke you just have to expel from your head, and you trust it will be cut from the show. But sometimes, if you're me, at least, you just say something stupid that could screw up everything, and, because you're playing with the pros, it all turns out maybe even funnier, by accident. This is what happened when food writer Mark Bittman came on the show:

PETER: So we're going to ask you three questions about Batman, specifically the movie, *Batman and Robin*. That was the one with George Clooney as Batman, and it is widely regarded as the very worst . . .

FAITH: Is that the one . . .

PETER: . . . of all the modern Batman films.

FAITH: Is that the one where Batman had nipples?

PETER: That is the one.

MARK BITTMAN: That answers the first question.

PETER: I am never inviting you back, Faith. Answer . . . TWO questions correctly, and you'll win our prize.

FAITH: Oh, my God, I'm so sorry. And that's all I know about it.

PETER: Yeah, thank you, Faith.

FAITH: I'm so sorry.

PETER: Well, we'll go through this anyway.

Peter was genuinely annoyed with me, which made it even funnier. Moments like those convince everyone the show is definitely not scripted.

After a taping, we take questions from the audience. Someone will often ask, "What's the funniest thing that ever happened that didn't make it on air?" Whereupon Peter will launch into a story about the episode that featured someone off to the side of the stage, signing for a few deaf audience members. A guest on that show described a difficult experience as being akin to "shitting a pineapple." Peter expertly demonstrates how the interpreter signed the shitting of a pineapple. Then we usually sign autographs, and I'm always freshly flattered when someone's psyched to take a picture with me, especially if she's eleven years old, and especially if I owe her parents an apology for the content of some of my jokes. Sometimes people tell me after a show that they really like my laugh. I love that. I laugh a lot when I'm on WWDTM. I giggle so often that I'm too busy to count how many laughs I might have provoked.

Is it too much to say this show has given me some real-life lessons? That sometimes you don't have to work so hard? And being fearless enough to sound stupid can pay off, and you don't always have to be the winner?

I can hear Peter Sagal answering me, wearily. "Yes. Yes, Faith, it's too much to say. It's just a comedy show, and you're even nerdier than the rest of us."

Buy Buy Hellmouth

l should have known it might not go too well the moment we decided to take separate trains to go downtown. What kind of newlywed couple expecting their first child doesn't travel together to pick out their baby stuff? But we were running late to meet our friend Tracy, who'd offered to meet us at Buy Buy Baby on a Saturday morning and tell us what we needed to purchase in order to become parents. I was freezing in the February wind as we stood outside the Lincoln Center subway stop while John suddenly had to make a call he didn't want me to overhear. So we, not altogether cheerfully, decided I'd hop on the next train, and John would follow after his mysterious call.

I expected Tracy to bring her husband, Sam, but I didn't anticipate finding her elementary school-aged son and daughter waiting with them, just inside the gigantic automatic doors of the Mecca for the fecund. My surprise highlighted the fact that I wasn't a mother yet, and therefore hadn't really considered that on weekends parents generally spend time with their children. They were generous about

my tardiness, but I was informed we were up against family
karate class in forty-five minutes. However, *Fortune Magazine* named Tracy one of the "World's 50 Greatest Leaders,"
so if anyone could guide us efficiently, it was she. I was ready
for a checklist, an inventory of items I could collect to as-
semble myself into a fantastic—or at least clueful—mother.
I brought pen and paper to take notes.

Tracy is a graceful, unprecious mother and a blunt
CEO. She's the type of person who gives a TED talk and
casually asks you, "Are you going to Davos this year?",
charitably implying you even understand what the World
Economic Forum is. To which I answer, out loud, "No, not
this year," and in my head I add, "Largely because, for me,
Davos is a knight in service to Stannis Baratheon, Lord of
Dragonstone."

John caught up with us in the middle of the baby clothes.
I gave him a kiss and grabbed his hand, wanting to push
the reset button on this exciting outing. In one of the many
parenting books I'd been marking up with notes, I'd learned
that marital satisfaction peaks during the third trimester of
a couple's first pregnancy. I was weeks shy of my third trimester. Except for the fact that we really weren't having sex
because John humbly feared he might impale our fetus, we
were pretty darn maritally satisfied. It was a good time to set
sail on our journey into a sea of onesies. I'd been anticipating
soft pastels, but I found myself swimming in neon pink and
purple for girls and a lot of chartreuse and brown for boys.
My son's potential layette featured monster trucks, gaping
T. Rexes, and suspiciously friendly sharks. I especially did
not want my boy to wear the onesie that proclaimed TOUGH
LIKE DADDY. I shuddered to think I could walk to the girls'

rack and find PUSSY LIKE MOMMY. Furthermore, I did not want him wearing clothes festooned with footballs. As a gangly adolescent, my husband experienced so many blows to his head playing football that the only realistic onesie for his kid would say, CONCUSSED LIKE DADDY. I await the out-fits that celebrate our family's de facto traits, such as PALE LIKE MOMMY and HALF JEWISH. We didn't linger.

Tracy eagerly marched us toward the breast corner and surveyed the display of breast pumps wistfully. "God, I miss breastfeeding," she told us all, causing her children to scat-ter. She turned to me and announced, "This is what they're made for. This is your breasts' time to shine!" I duly wrote in my notebook, "breasts—time to shine." The last time my breasts shone was when I guest-starred on a Roger Corman TV show with two Playmates. (The Playmates were women, not what I nicknamed my boobs.) I was part of a nefarious duo named Bend and Stretch. Being the shorter criminal, I played Bend. Being the only actress sans breast implants, the wardrobe lady had to shove a total of four of those squishy chicken cutlet things into my push-up bra just to make me look like I belonged in this pneumatic, vice-riddled world.

Tracy strongly suggested the Medela Pump in Style. I wasn't sure how one actually pumps stylishly—is it a matter of technique or flattering flange size? I looked at all the parts and was too intimidated to ask how it works or when to use it. Tracy registered my consternation and assured me I'd fig-ure it out. I did not appreciate her confidence in me. I don't like being told I'll figure something out. I'm taking notes be-cause I want it figured out now please, especially something that involves my body being sucked into a machine. I prayed there was a Genius Bar for breast pumps. We discussed at length whether to get a backpack-carry pump or an over the shoulder. When I turned to seek John's input, I spied him playing with stuffed animals. I was already learning that motherhood is an exercise in gut-led solo decisions. I went for the shoulder strap. Check.

I summoned John for our introduction to several different "bottle systems." I'd just thought there were baby bottles. I had no idea I'd have to commit to a *system*. Dr. Brown's, Playtex, Born Free, Evenflo—most of them sounded like feminine hygiene products, so I gravitated toward the one that didn't. Then our guide delivered more shocking news: she warned us that our baby might reject the nipples we offer him. At first I panicked, because there's not much I can do about my nipples, although I have been known to cover them with Band-Aids when going braless. Then I realized we were talking about the nipples that come with the bottles. Effectively I learned that we might end up chucking the whole nonreturnable, nonrefundable *system* because a <u>baby</u> might demonstrate an irrational discrimination in nipples. I sent a message to my uterus: *You'll take the nipples I give you and you'll like them. Because I'm your mother, that's why.* How could I anticipate my child's teat preference? I looked deep into John's eyes and said, "Dr. Brown's? Do we just go for it?" We went for it, mostly because Tracy was ready to move. So we sped past the bottle warmers, breast milk bags, bottle sterilizers, nipple cream, nursing pillows, nipple shields, and areola cozies as she breezily waved her hand in their direction and said, "You can worry about those later." I was worried now. I was engorged with worry. Nothing about the words *nipple shield* sounded pleasant or even nonviolent.

John was gone again. I'd pictured us ambling through the store, holding hands all the while, possibly stopping to give each other soulful looks every time we picked out something that would cosset our son. As I strode past the registry center, I noticed unlined couples sitting with their "Registry Consultants," like lovebirds happily building a nest, twig by overpriced twig. How did they know what they wanted? I envied them their togetherness, not just the way they were side by side, but also the way they seemed to have their shit together. They looked cheerful and confident, with a shared buoyancy we were lacking. Or maybe it was a blood sugar thing. Neither John nor I had eaten breakfast.

Tracy escorted us through the monitor center, a.k.a. Fearmongering Central. We chose a monitor expensive enough to make us feel like good parents who didn't want their child to die of lack of surveillance but not so spendy that we felt like total chumps. My father, based on his reliably lackluster memory of my early years, tells me that he thinks he and my mother had a monitor, but only for sound. I feel cheated knowing that my folks weren't constantly willing me to keep breathing by visual means like decent, loving parents of today. The only benign residents of that department were a row of sleepy stuffies—sleep-inducing sound machines implanted inside cuddly surrogates. Once again, I found John moonily clutching a few of the animals. John, with a handicapped sister, didn't get much attention as a boy, and he'd explained that his stuffed animals were real friends to him. One day when he was about twelve, he discovered his father had unceremoniously thrown out all his stuffed animals "to make more room in the house." Seeing my husband like that, smiling gently while cradling

something small and cute, gave me a glimpse of the daddy
I hoped he'd be. Which was the type of father he never had.

There was no time for an earnest family meeting about
whether to register for the Sleep Sheep or Gentle Giraffe.
We'd been late; family karate class was nigh. We went with
sheep, the obvious choice.

We breezed past mysterious, bright things called Boppys,
Bumbos, and Gyminis as Tracy hustled us all down the stairs.
Fittingly, as we entered the bowels of the store, she and Sam
introduced us to "the shitters." A shitter, they explained to
us, in front of their mortified children, is what they named
the bouncing, vibrating, music-playing, automatic-rocking
contraption that unfailingly induced intestinal movement.
According to them, this was not optional. I nodded obedi-
ently and jotted down, "shitter." No time to stop and decide
between the Snugabunny or Rainforest Friends. I looked at
John with a mix of weariness and panic. My blood pressure
was rising as my glucose fell. For me, choosing the very first
things that would surround a miniperson I hadn't met—the
most important person in the world for whom I would be
100 percent responsible—felt momentous. I really didn't
know if he should be looking at dangling birdies or dangling
monkeys. "Choose later," Tracy urged, and we entered the
most confusing department of all: the Stroller Vortex.*

I turned to John and said, "You choose," and abandoned

---

* We returned to the Stroller Vortex again and then tested out strollers at two more stores. I grilled friends about their strollers for weeks
and fell down the rabbit hole of online customer reviews: "Bugaboo vs.
City Mini." Scoff if you must, but when you don't have a car or even
parking for your stroller, because your husband's dog takes up valuable floor space, this shit matters.

him during his tutorial with Sam and Tracy. Daddy could decide on things with wheels—I decided then and there that I would carry my child in a sling and breastfeed him lissomely while walking down the street. Plus I forgot to mention that, at the time of this excursion, I had not yet capitulated to maternity clothes, so a severe camel toe was effecting a private punishment. I walked like John Wayne over to the room devoted to recliners and sank into one. I put my feet on a nursing footstool. Did you know there are nursing footstools? I didn't. Something else I needed to get, or else I would be breastfeeding my child at a suboptimal angle. I closed my eyes and tried not to cry in front of Tracy's kids, who were vigorously testing the structural integrity of the chairs.

It was all too, too much. It had taken my whole life to get here and now it was too rushed. This baby was coming too soon. I had willfully ignored this ineluctable need to gear up just as I'd been in denial about needing maternity clothes. Don't get me wrong, I'd always wanted to be a mother. I felt intensely lucky. But at forty, I wasn't ready. I wasn't ready because I was forty, because being forty meant I'd lived a long time as just me, as someone who could fairly well do what she pleased, and I'd created—finally, after a lot of hard work and luck—a life that did please me, immensely. And at forty I was old enough, and had seen enough, to know that this baby would change everything forever. The sheer amount of crap in that hellhole proved it to me. That one teeny baby could require so much stuff filled me with terror.* Not

---

* Buy Buy Baby puts a more positive spin on it, on its website: "*Who knew such a tiny bundle of love could need so much stuff?*"

because of the expense of it all, which is admittedly offensive, not because our "nursery" would be the room where we had our desk, printer, and John's humidors, but because of the undeniable necessity of it all: my child will need so much, and I have to give it to him. Also because of the expectation—if I don't furnish him with the best, I'm shortchanging him. I don't mean in a competitive, consumptive way—I never cared about having the blingest stroller or the $3,500 Lucite crib. I mean that you want to give your kid the finest things that will help him grow and thrive and comfortably eliminate waste in a vibrating seat that plays a jazz version of "Frère Jacques."

I felt that we were in a kind of hell. A fluorescent-lit capitalistic hellmouth of choices. There's a phenomenon identified by psychologists and economists. They call it "the paradox of choice" or "analysis paralysis." Basically it says that the more choices we have, the less happy we are. Too much information is debilitating. I believe this, even if it makes for a strong argument for arranged marriage. I was paralyzed in that Lac-T-Girl recliner. Every item on our registry represented something I didn't know about the most challenging thing I would ever do, and that frightened me. This flaming abyss was a lesson in how much I had to get and how much I had to give up.

What I know now is that you can't possibly figure out what's best for your child ahead of time. Most of the junk you buy doesn't matter—as long as bottles and bottoms are clean, and you put your baby to sleep on his back, it will all work out. And what works for your child this week won't be necessary next week. Nipples get rejected.

(I will say this, though: Get the wipes warmer and the

Snotsucker. I know you're thinking that kids today have it too easy and how, back in our day, babies walked uphill in the snow both ways with cold butt cheeks. But warm wipes feel really good on everyone involved in the fecal maintenance business. And NoseFrida the Snotsucker? This is not a villain in a Pixar movie; it evacuates mucus. Like out of your kid's brain. It's a tube you put in your mouth connected to a kind of syringe thing that you insert into your baby's nose. And then you suck. Ignore the one-star reviewer on Amazon who reports, "I suck and suck and her boogers barely move," to which I say, dude, please get your COPD checked out. Even your baby will appear shocked at its efficacy. I use that thing with a zeal that verges on child abuse. It's from Sweden, and though it's not sexy or cute, you should get one.)

A Romanian facialist gave me the best advice I ever received when I was pregnant. When someone is looking at your skin under a magnifying glass, you feel a strong sense of intimacy with her. So I confessed how anxious I felt about not knowing how to take care of a baby, and she offered me these simple words: *Your son will teach you how to be his mama.* This brought tears to my eyes not caused by extractions from my pores. And she was right: there was nothing I could really do ahead of time, no gadget I could buy that would prepare me, say, for the fact that my now three-year-old will not go to sleep unless we hug and kiss his stuffed excavator and then place exactly four blankets, in a particular order, *over my son's head.*

But I didn't know all this then, sprawled out in the center of the netherworld, completely stultified.

And that is where our Virgil left us. Tracy and her karate

kids had guided us as far as they could. Unlike Dante, we had to climb out of the inferno alone.

John joined me in the recliner section. Dazed by the alpha wake, we stared at each other silently. We were not going through this experience as a team even though we were similarly enervated. I dispatched John to find a salesperson to talk to about baby furniture and let a few tears slide as I sat in the puffy lavender recliner that looked very '80s. I have a soft spot in my heart for this recliner, because it now lives in our bedroom. In it, I have spent countless hours reading stories to my kids and writing this book. But that first time I sat in it, I wept. Tracy was gone, so I could finally snivel. And oh, the hunger. I longed for a Diaper Genie to grant me one wish of a Luna bar.

When John returned, it was an excellent time for a brief, intense fight. We were both so shell-shocked and bitchy, it was inevitable. We decided to compare levels of fatigue and hunger. This was a bad move on John's part. He was outnumbered, two to one. Because when I said, "You have no idea how exhausted and starving I am," and he replied, "I'm just as tired and hungry as you are," my only option was to break the news that I WAS THE ONE GESTATING ANOTHER HUMAN BEING, A HUMAN BEING HE MADE WITH HIS PENIS. There's not much a man can say when you remind him that you're pregnant, and he will never ever understand how you feel. It was a trump card I played only once, flung down in the fiery maws of the hellmouth.

We left to meet our friend Sharon for tea, to look at photo books she'd made of our wedding. I sat there, sipping herbal something with no Splenda, contemplating how far away the wedding seemed. Just four months earlier, we were breathlessly—possibly nauseatingly—in love, full of passion and hope. You could see it in the photos she showed us, taken all over Rome, from the Forum to the Villa Borghese Park. Beaming in front of the fountain in Piazza Navona in my wedding dress, embraced by my new husband, I looked care- and camel-toe-free. I thanked Sharon for her beautiful work while John stayed largely silent and got to drink caffeine.

We were not peaking, John and I. If we aren't peaking now, I wondered, have we already peaked? If it's this stressful now, how will I ever be a mother to a baby who lives outside of me?

Two days later, John took me maternity clothes shopping and sat patiently through an unsexy fashion show. A week later, he gave me a Valentine's Day present of a special photo he'd had repaired and framed for me. That morning we'd been running late for Buy Buy Baby, I learned, he'd been on the phone with the framers trying to straighten out my gift they'd botched.

Since climbing out of that pit, I'm relieved to say that we've experienced countless peaks and valleys, and I can only assume they'll keep on coming. That's parenthood; that's marriage; that's life.

Just be sure to have a baby with someone who will go with you to hell and back.

On the Fringe: A Cautionary Tale

Whenever I hear a recovering addict confess of booze or cocaine, "I miss it every day," I totally understand, because that's how I feel about eyelash extensions. For two years and two months I batted lush, long, dark, curly, PERFECT lashes. Not a day goes by that I don't wish I could still flutter them.

Can lashes change your life? Yes, depending on who applies them.

I'm a little afraid to tally exactly how much I spent on my lashes during that time. Let's just say that I could have kept a small public radio station in one of the Dakotas from having to do pledge drives for a year.

It all began as I'm pretty sure most of these dark journeys do: a phone call with a stranger possessing a thick Russian accent who promised to give me what I need. Her name was Karina, and when I told her what I do for a living—that is, hope that if people are listening to me they are simultaneously finding me slightly attractive, even on the radio—she assured me that she knew exactly what to do. I'd found her after watching Kathy Lee and Hoda Lucy-and-Ethel their way through a lesson on "Lash Dip" with their beauty expert. This was back in the days when I would turn on the fourteenth hour of the *Today* show and let its frantic drunken song fill the apartment while I wasted more time than I ever knew I had. Nowadays the TV is never on before dark, because science warns me that if my young children pass by a live television screen, they will become violent and obese and believe that Crunch Berries occur in nature. Lash Dip sounded great—better than guacamole—a no-commitment dunk in gunk that would make your lashes dark for a few weeks so you didn't have to use mascara. When I googled Lash Dip, I found out Karina was a local purveyor. I e-mailed her. She said this warranted a phone call. She talked me out of the dip immediately (won't curl, will clump—and "clump" sounds really ominous in a Russian accent) and assured me that what I wanted were lash extensions. "Dey vil be beautiful. Hew vil loff dem."

I'd never seen convincing, noncheesy lash extensions. They always looked very stripper cum Snuffleupagus to me. But Karina insisted, "Trust me," and if you've ever seen a Bond movie, you understand that there's something irresistible about a sexy Russian voice demanding your trust. Turned out, when I met her in person, that Karina is hot enough to be a Bond girl, with a license to beautify. She has a perfect body, which I think might be aided by breast extensions. It can be a slippery slope once you start extending yourself.

So I put my eyes in her hands, and I lay down on her table, and thus began two beautiful relationships. One between me and my lash extensions and the other between me and Karina.

The whole thing took about two hours. During that time, I bonded with Karina as immediately as the extensions did with my lashes. I told her about my boyfriend John and how I wanted to start a family. She told me how much she loved *Sunday Morning* and her two kids and husband. We agreed that Jewish guys are the best. Finally I was allowed to open my eyes, which were stinging from glue fumes. I saw Karina peering down at me, drying my lashes with a miniature fan in her hand—the kind gals "going through the change" use at the gym. She gave my face a studied appraisal and then declared, "*Kukla.*" *Kukla*, she explained, means "doll" in Russian.

When I got up from her magic table and looked in the mirror, I was astonished. My eyes appeared bigger than ever, framed stunningly as promised. The lashes were black and curly and splayed in a classily unnatural way, which was fine with me since I wasn't exactly whipping out my Visa to achieve the natural look.

They also distracted from my skin. I have a flawful complexion. Just ask the woman who, after seeing me on CNN—where I opined that a pregastric bypass Chris Christie should lose weight for health reasons—e-mailed to inquire, "You know, your skin looks pretty rough, so why don't you fix THAT???" I've always gazed at women with beautiful skin wondering if they have any notion how lucky they are, especially that they can wear red lipstick, which is one of my unattainable life goals right up there with achieving a reliable vaginal orgasm and cutting back on salt.

Having a constantly lackluster complexion is embarrassing and humbling, especially when you're on camera. Extra especially when you've heard a director whisper to his DP (director of photography) about you, "Don't worry—we'll fix it in post." My new kuklashes were fixed in pre. They drew invaluable attention to my eyes.

It took a little while for me to accept them as part of my face. A day after application, I caught sight of myself in a window near Fifth Avenue. My hair was in a ponytail, I was wearing workout clothes with a Nike puffer jacket and thought maybe I looked like a chorus girl running errands in between her matinee and evening performances. I wondered if everyone was looking at me thinking I was a hussy with a fringe on top.

John never mentioned them. A few days after I got the extensions, we were on his sofa watching *The Social Network*. At some point, I ended up snuggling on top of him and he murmured, "Pretty eyes." I had to make sure he knew. "The lashes aren't mine, you know." "I know," he said. "I don't care, I'm talking about your green eyes."

We never talked about them again until they came off.

At the root of it all, I just wanted to be naturally pretty. Of course it makes no rational sense that fake eyelashes made me feel naturally pretty, but they did. It wasn't just their convenience, even though I saved at least fifteen minutes a day not having to deal with my demanding eyelash habit. My system involved curling naked, pale, Anglo-Saxon lashes, brushing loose powder on them, applying one coat of curling mascara, waiting for it to dry, optional reapplication of powder, more curling, another coat of volumizing mascara. Assiduous declumping and wiping away smudges with Q-tips followed. Recurling throughout the day advised. I curled so much I could have qualified for the Canadian Winter Olympics team.

Lash extensions let me swan about, pretending I had effortlessly beautiful eyes. Strangers told me so; friends interrupted conversations to say, "Your lashes are so amazing, I can't concentrate." The extensions were there when I woke up, they were there on my makeup-less face at the gym, they were there when I sat in the makeup chair before going on camera. They were there when I cried through two miscarriages, one wedding, and one birth.

Two months after I met Karina, I fairly floated into her room at the salon in an Upper East Side town house.

"So . . ." I said, as I slipped off my shoes, smiling like the Cheshire Cat. "I'm pregnant."

"Hewaaat? Oh my Got. Baby. I em so heppy for yew. But yew should not tell peepul. Eets too soon."

"How could I lie here for an hour and not tell you? Anyway, I don't believe in jinxing good news."

But she was right. I had to untell too many people about the loss of my first pregnancy.

That wasn't the first time Karina was right. Karina was right about *everything*.

Karina's wisdom changed me. It didn't just change me because she gave me invaluable guidance; no, she was a lesson in not judging a book by its cover or vocation. I was surprised that a person who focused on faces could be so deep. I do recognize that this was obnoxious of me since I, in fact, met Karina solely because I was paying her to improve my face. Because her calling was cosmetic, I did not expect her to be so smart (fluency in three languages and degrees in music and gemology), and I did not expect her to be so wise. I feel ashamed now about my superficial presumption. Which is the same way I feel thinking back to when I found out I was having a boy.

"So it's a boy," I said to Karina, sighing as I settled in for the touch-up.

"Det's purrfict."

"I know I'm so lucky to be having any kind of baby," I said, "but I always wanted a girl."

"Boy is purrfict for your ferst. Den he can be beek bruh-dair," she replied as she commenced yanking old glue off old fake lashes.

"But what if I never have another baby, what if I never get my girl?"

"I know hew vant your gerril but beleef me, Faithy, hew vil fall in loff with your boy. Hew vil loff him so much hew vil forget about John. I was so fet for a whole year after I hed Alex, hew would not haff beleeft it and I did not vant my husband to touch me anyvay."

"How were you fat? You were breastfeeding—that's supposed to make you skinny."

"Det is such a bunch of bullsheet, excuse me. Ven hew are breastfeeding, hew are a cow. Ecktuelly a cow. Hew don't loos deh veight until hew stop, I'm tellink hew."

She was right. I am crazy about my son, and breastfeed-ing makes you eat like a trucker ordering his last meal on death row.

One day Karina and I didn't talk at all. I shuffled in,

hugged her, hopped onto the table, arranged my growing belly to my left side so as not to impede blood flow to my placenta and shut my eyes.

With her hands on my face, my friend said, "Hew juss sleep, baby."

Karina fixed my extensions two days before Augustus arrived. I was completely naked when I gave birth, wearing only my lashes. My doula* took a photo of me, holding my son, covered in our collective goo. I'm crying from happiness. My eyes, as I gaze down on my tiny boy, look gorgeous.

The only thing I'll never know whether Karina was right about was her advice regarding how to conceive a girl.

"Listen to me: when hew'r ovulatink, hew must make a douche with lemon just before hew heff sex. I know diss sounds crazy but I'm tellink hew it verks, eet's how I got my Julia."

I'll never know because I wasn't up for a citron *pressé* in the vadge.

My sessions with Karina kept me sane. I didn't need to go to therapy.

I didn't need to "see someone" because I was seeing Karina, by which I mean not seeing her for ninety minutes every three weeks. Three weeks was as long as it took for a couple of my spider-leggy lashes to wilt downward and just dangle, leaving me looking like a soused prostitute in a Toulouse

---

* The word *doula* comes from an ancient Greek word meaning "female servant," but in modern days, they're women to whom you pay a lot of drachmas to help you through labor. You can then give certain relatives another reason to roll their eyes when you drop things like, "My doula is coming over tonight to explain birth stations of presentation using a doll and a turtleneck."

Lautrec painting. I can't really describe the reapplication process, because I didn't want to know how the sausage was made. I invariably felt some tugging and trusted she wasn't pulling my real eyelashes out by the roots.

"How are hew, baby?"

I closed my eyes to begin. Her iPhone always played a relaxing Pandora station.

"Oh, Karina. I mean, big picture, fine, nobody's dying and we can pay the rent. Little picture, it sucks. Augustus doesn't eat, and John and I are not very nice to each other. How do people do this?? I have only one kid and it's so hard and I want to have another! What's wrong with me?"

"Let me tell hew somedink," she said. "It vil suck for . . . five years."

"Five YEARS?"

"I'm sorry, baby, but it's true. Hew vil get your gerril and hew vil be exhosted and vil fight more with John, and in about five years dee sun vil shine and hew vil feel like hew agen."

She had to cancel our appointment once because her mother had died suddenly in Moscow. When she returned, we talked about it. I mostly listened. While my eyes were closed, I felt something wet on my face. It was Karina's tear.

"Oh, I'm sorry," she sniffled.

"Please don't be sorry," I said. "I love hearing about your mom."

I was deeply sad for her but glad she was able to cry with me.

So why did I ever, ever unlash myself? There were practical reasons. I didn't think I could pull off the maintenance time commitment with a ton of new work and imminent fertility treatments. I wanted to see my son more than look pretty. But there were more spiritual reasons. I'd forgotten what I really looked like. When you're a little scared to see what you really look like, it's probably time to face the truth of your face. And I'd lost another pregnancy. After that so-bering denouement, it seemed like the right time to strip something else away.

My fertility doctor had advised us to travel as a way to heal physically and emotionally before starting another round of IVF, so we were about to go to France. I figured I could have Karina take off the extensions, and I'd hide in Paris for a week where I could learn to tie a scarf in such a soigné way that no one would notice my lack of lash. Surely a week was enough time for lashes to grow in fully.

Karina took them off in a remarkably brief session. I was afraid to look, so I tried to read her face.

A small smile.

"Is it horrible?" I asked.

"No, baby," she said.

So I turned to face the mirror.

I was shocked. I wasn't ready for the fallout. I didn't expect beauty, but I also didn't expect a kukla with facial alopecia. My top lashes were stubs. The roots were all there, but there was no there there. No hairs that grew out and up, however modestly—it was as if someone or something, like the Vanity Fairy, had taken tiny little scissors and made a blunt cut about one-eighth of an inch from my eyelid. I put my hands to my cheeks, looking more Munch's *The Scream* than *Home Alone*. The first thing I said was the only thought in my head: "Oh my God, I look like my mother before she died."

My mother didn't really have much of a choice when it came to chemotherapy stripping her of her lashes. But I had chosen this, and my inner Catholic girl felt like it was punishment. I was Icarus: I had flown too close to the sun and scorched off my fringe.

My bottom lashes were three times as long as my top lashes. This is a cute look only if you're Raggedy Ann.

"Hew loog pretty. Dey are dair. Dey are short but dey are dair," Karina assured me. "Hew loog fresh in a vay."

She gave me a vial of something called Lash Food. I would have taken hemlock.

"Dey vil grow beck. Geef eet few months."

The removal of my lashes—which were never completely mine—so humbled me that I didn't want to see anyone, much less myself. I wore my sunglasses a lot and avoided mirrors. It reminded me of how I feel about once every seven years when one of the veneers on my two front teeth pops off, and I have to face up to the fact that my real front teeth are now whittled nubs that make me look like an Ozarkian crank addict.

No matter how many times I tried to get John to admit I looked like a chemo patient, he refused. "I don't look at parts of you," he'd insist, like a perfectly evolved husband who also never notices when I get my hair done or have large pieces of skin flaking off after a facial peel. We went to Paris, and I focused on the way the light in Sainte-Chapelle shone down on my son on his first birthday. I stockpiled unpasteurized *fromage* in my fat cells, hoping a new pregnancy would soon make it off-limits.

And my eyelashes did grow back over ten months, at

approximately the same rate as the daughter I began to
grow, with the help of science rather than lemon juice.

I do not look beautiful in pictures with my newborn daughter. When you have babies in your forties, you are constantly
and dramatically confronted with your aging. In photos, my
babies' perfect skin poses next to my bumpy, wrinkly, spotted
technically-old-enough-to-be-their-grandma skin. In the rare
photos of Minerva's first year in which I appear—in contrast
to my presence in photos from her older brother's first year—I
have no lash extensions to balance out my crow's-feet.

There _is_ a postextension photo I truly love. I love it because it surprised me. My brother took it the Thanksgiving when I was five months' pregnant with Minerva, and
our little family of three and a half people was walking on
the beach. I was in sweats, not wearing a lick of makeup,
which is usual for a holiday with my family. But I remember thinking—when David took the picture—_I wish I'd at
least put on some mascara for Thanksgiving Day._ The picture
turned out beautiful—of all of us. Simple. Happy. Real.
Burgeoning with things to come, a kukla inside me.

When I use mascara now, I apply it to such dramatic effect that my children often reach out to touch my eyelashes,
in wonder of how different I look with three to four coats
of its "K-Polymer formula with a lipid complex of abyssinia
oil and pseudo-ceramid." In fact, "Mommy wears mascara
on her eyes" were my son's very first words to Santa when
I took him for his inaugural visit to Macy's Santaland. He
thrice announced this to Santa and his elves before we left
to let the next little Jewish child have a turn.

I was never sheepish about devoting so much energy and
money to my eyelash extensions. Maybe it was the Oscar

Wildean side of me that believes "It is only the shallow people who do not judge by appearances," or maybe it was because it was all tax-deductible. But what surprised me was the depth my frivolous endeavor could yield.

Now, almost three years later, I miss Karina much more than I miss my lashes. Karina and I still text, and we're always trying to make a plan to meet, but we haven't for a long time. After I had Minerva, Karina offered me the gift of a facial multiple times, and I simply could not find the two hours to get across town and into her hands.

I miss going to great lengths to take care of myself. I miss that quiet hour with my friend.

Her most recent text read:

> *Your babies are so so precious and remind yourself that you got the perfect family you always dreamt about, beautiful boy and a girl and a husband who loves you and actually does help with the kids. She is so big, our baby Minushka! Miss you, please get your butt out to swim and tan in our semi-furnished backyard.*

The glue has set between Karina and me.

Book Marked

My first memory is of sitting with my mother in a white rocking chair with a pink gingham cushion as she reads me *The Giving Tree*. In the book, an apple tree gives herself to a boy as he grows up—first her branches for swinging, then her apples for selling, next her limbs for building a house, and finally her trunk for a boat in which he can sail away. In the end, the lad—now an old man—returns, and the tree can only offer him her stump as a place to rest. This tree is the ultimate woodland approval junkie: here's all of me; use me, love me. At the end of the book, my mother's voice breaks, and she wipes her eyes. But I am maybe three, and I do not understand how a story—told mostly in pictures—about a tree and a boy moves her to tears. On her lap, I feel happy. She is the giving; I am the given to. I have not yet gone to college to take Women's Studies 101 and recognize the tree's gender-predictable self-abnegation. I have not yet become a parent-stump to my own emotionally ax-wielding child. So I do not yet grasp that Shel Silverstein's genius lies in telling the story of parenting as an arboresque fable, be-

cause if he didn't get all poetic about it, the real title of a
children's book about parenting would be *This Shit Is Hard
as Shit*.

Even though it took me almost forty years to learn it, my
mother gave me this one book as a lesson.

My father, on the other hand, gave me countless books
as a lifelong conversation.

I didn't talk with him the way I talked with my mom—
easily and about everything. My mother was effusive. If I
got the lead in a play, she might have clapped, beamed, and
clutched her heart, saying, "I just don't know how I got a
daughter like you!" My father, on the other hand, faced,
perhaps, with one of my report cards, would deliver this,
very calmly:

"I'm impressed but not surprised."

It's not accurate to call him a man of few words. He's
articulate and witty, learned and opinionated. But he's not
social, and he's not chatty. He's a man of select words who
loves words. Books helped us say things to each other. Books
with plots that have nothing to do with your life can still say
I understand you, or I want you to understand me. When
your father says read this, he can also be saying this story
moved me, or this one changed the way I viewed the world
when I was your age, or I believe you're mature enough to
handle what this author wants you to know.

That's how I found myself, one night between seventh
and eighth grade, wide awake and frozen with fear. I was
sitting in our living room, in the dimmest light, after my
whole family had gone to bed. I'd just finished *The Turn of
the Screw* by Henry James, a summer read prescribed to me
by my father, the doctor of philosophy. I'd requested this

assignment, because I wanted to demonstrate I was ready to
matriculate to reading "literature" from reading *Sweet Valley
High*, and so my father suggested some Gothic psychological horror. Even though its terrifying last sentence left me
unable to move, I couldn't wait till the next morning to tell
my dad I'd actually been able to follow James's seemingly
infinite clauses to the end of his eternal sentences.

"Dad, I finished it last night. Oh my GOSH. You didn't
warn me!"

His eyebrows shot up in delighted cahoots. "How about
that ending, huh?"

And we parsed the ending and what it could mean, and
our discussion concluded with my asking, "What do I read
next?"

He gave me a Jane Austen anthology, and I fell for Elizabeth Bennet—granted, as clichéd a rite of passage for a
bookish teenager as buying your first tube of Clearasil, but
nonetheless a love affair. When I mentioned I liked e. e.
cummings, mostly due to my adolescent admiration for his
f u to capitalization, Dad found a cummings collection. He
didn't judge my nascent taste. I think of how he must have
driven his pimpy-looking Chrysler New Yorker to the bookstore to buy his daughter a book of poetry; I think of him
inscribing it with his pointy penmanship and asking Mom
to wrap it for me as a gift.

I feel like I bonded with my father through words and
writing and books from the beginning of my life, since the
rat-a-tat-tat of his typewriter lulled me to sleep as a little
girl. He was writing his PhD draft, and the syncopated beat
of its composition connected me to him in the way that the
swishing rhythm of the womb attunes a baby to her mother.

Our cadence was not without interruption, however. Once, when I was sleepily singing "Rubber Ducky" to the backup drumming of his typewriter keys, my dad came into my room and asked me to be quiet. That kind of bummed me out. Then again, there are a few things my dad did that I wouldn't do, such as smoke Marlboro reds while driving his family around in a sealed Chinook camper, playing a Roger Whittaker eight-track.

He was pursuing his doctorate while teaching English at the public high school he'd attended a decade before. Very *Welcome Back, Kotter.* (If this reference is lost on you, try to imagine a time when John Travolta had a lot of hair that was real.) He was writing a treatise on the beginnings of women's education at the Harvard Annex, which became Radcliffe College. He did this at night, probably after grading thirty-five essays on the grooviness of Holden Caulfield in *The Catcher in the Rye.* My dad was the son of two humble people who never made it past tenth grade. He worked hard to achieve his advanced degrees, even harder than he'd worked to lose his Boston accent.

As a toddler, I liked to help him get dressed for work, in the dark, rushed hours of the morning. It made me feel important, especially when I got to pick out his socks. This meant he occasionally discovered he was wearing two different-colored socks while presenting himself as an authority figure to students not much younger than he was. One morning, outfitted by *moi* in a double-breasted blazer, tight tattersall bell-bottoms, and a yellow clip-on bow tie, he no doubt swaggered into his first period AP English class. He had a lot going on with such a getup, and I'm sure he'd also paid some attention to his longish hair and beard-mustache combo. He must have taken a moment to smooth his side-burns. That his copious hair situation surely took some of his focus will become meaningful in a moment.

On this particular day, he was teaching Thoreau's *Walden*. He led a discussion about how Thoreau ventures out to the frozen middle of Walden Pond to commune with the great eye in the sky. The marks Thoreau chips into the ice create a kind of cross. My father, who probably should have been an actor, wanted to dramatize the symbolism of Thoreau's excursion. So he turned his back to the class, unbuttoned all four hundred buttons on his double-breasted blazer, and flung his arms out in cruciform as he spun abruptly around.

A girl in the front row let out a little scream.

His fly was wide open.

The bell rang. My father bolted to the vice principal's office before any traumatized teenagers could get there first. He confessed to Vice Principal Piccirilli that he'd exposed himself to his class in the name of literary symbolism. He explained that inviting his three-year-old daughter to be his stylist early in the morning meant he sometimes missed a step, like zipping his pants.

Evidently, my father was so passionate about literature that sometimes he literally couldn't contain himself.

Upon request, my father will tell this story. I love hearing it, a little bit because I'm the guest star, but mostly because I like seeing him come alive as he falls back into teacher mode and reenacts his Thoreau lecture. He left that profession before I entered first grade, but I know he was an inspired teacher, because he basically taught me. As he drove me to afternoon auditions and rehearsals, he'd hold book club on wheels. When I was reading *The Scarlet Letter* by

Nathaniel Hawthorne, my father would ask me questions like, "What does it mean for Hester to remove her cap and let her hair fall?" We'd discuss Puritanism and its effect on women. "Why do you think Hester's love child's name is Pearl?" We'd talk about how a pearl is made—a natural irritation, something accidentally lodged into the belly of the oyster that grows into a wild jewel. Suddenly I appreciated Hawthorne's genius. Perhaps the great Nate gets a little obvi when it comes to assigning symbolic names to other characters, like gloomy DIMmesdale and the villainous CHILL-INGworth, but high school sophomores should thank him for throwing them a bone across the centuries.

I had a different high school English teacher who showed far less faith in my literary comprehension than my father did. *Great Expectations* marked my first encounter with Dickens in more ways than one: I had my own great expectations that Mrs. Altman was going to appreciate my essay on the novel. I worked on it all weekend, crafting the requisite five paragraphs. I was really proud of this paper, not only because I used a thesaurus to learn the word *incarceration*, but also because my dad read it before I turned it in and told me I'd done a good job. When Mrs. Altman handed out graded essays to everyone but me and asked if I'd see her after class, I wondered if she wanted to congratulate me personally on the deployment of my new sparkle word. Instead, she informed me she detected the strong odor of CliffsNotes in my writing.

When I came home from school and told my dad he should expect a call from my English teacher, he appeared simultaneously pissed and proud. It never crossed his mind to ask me if I'd cheated. He was far more pleased to express to Mrs. Altman his steadfast confidence in me than he was even to disabuse her of the insane notion that his home might be infested with CliffsNotes. I remember the serious eagerness with which he awaited her call. I heard him greet my teacher in a low, measured tone. I followed him as he walked upstairs with the gigantic cordless phone to my parents' bedroom. He had a glint in his eye as he shut the door and cleared his throat. The next day, Mrs. Altman mutely handed me a paper marked with nothing but a scarlet letter A and then lectured the class on plagiarism. Maybe he told her she shouldn't be surprised if she'd been impressed with my paper.

I astonished no one by ultimately choosing to study literature in college and grad school. My linear seventeen-year-old mind had, at first, decided that, because I wanted to continue acting, I should study theater in college. Rejected by all the best schools to which I applied, I majored in drama at my "safety school" and hated every minute of it. Freshman year, I went home for Thanksgiving, feeling anything but grateful, complaining to my parents that I wasn't learning what I wanted to in college. I had to take classes where professors taught me things like how to pronounce words like "Tuesday" with a "liquid U": "tee-yew-sday." This comes in handy only if you order tuna salad a lot. One midterm involved lip-synching something from *The Little Mermaid*. I was Ursula, and I killed, but it wasn't enough for me. Dad suggested, simply, "Why don't you apply to Harvard?" That idea, that school, had never occurred to me. I thought I was too artsy; I also thought I'd never get in, since several of Harvard's Ivy League sisters had turned me down.

But I applied, and I did get in. I was more surprised than my dad.

I embraced Victorian literature as a transfer student. When I called my father to inform him I'd finally finished *Bleak House*, and that he was right, it was just about the greatest novel ever, he sounded so gratified. "Oh, just wait till you read *Our Mutual Friend*," he said, keeping our book club going.

One day, as I was researching a paper on suffragettes in the Schlesinger Library in Radcliffe Yard, I stumbled across my father's dissertation. I held in my hand the book that had provided the soundtrack of my earliest youth. It was small and fat. I flipped to the back to see how many people had checked it out over a decade and a half. Hardly anyone, which I decided not to tell him. I wondered, as I flipped through its dusty pages and regarded its old-fashioned font, did my dad ever dream his daughter might grow up to be a part of the place he wrote about? Maybe he did or maybe he didn't, but I felt like my presence in that library that day, holding his book, made me its coda.

In grad school, in England, I ventured beyond my father's canon. Fired up by my college-bred feminism, I read everything that Virginia Woolf ever wrote, just as she was meant to be read: in Doc Martens. I traveled, not just through stories, but by planes and trains, even on camels and elephants, to places my father had never been.

When I returned from overseas, it was time for me to give *him* a book.

You see, not long after I came back, Mom died. We didn't have much time to figure out what to say at her funeral. We'd known she was dying, but who prepares the right words in advance? I bookmarked a passage in Virginia Woolf's posthumous essay collection, *Moments of Being*. I gave lines to my father that Woolf had composed about losing her mother. He read them at my mother's service. He read them carefully, but with no less passion than he'd once used to inspire his students.

The dead, so people say, are forgotten, or they should rather say, that life has for the most part little significance to any of us. But now and again on more occasions than I can number, in bed at night, or in the street, or as I come into the room, there she is; beautiful, emphatic, with her familiar phrase and her laugh; closer than any of the living are, lighting our random lives as with a burning torch, infinitely noble and delightful to her children.

Then and now, the first image in my head of my mother is always of her emphatic signature move. She'd clap her hands together and hold them, clasped, as she shook her head with a big toothy smile. She was so liberal with this gesture that it's a wonder you always felt special for having produced such delight.

I have lived now almost twenty years without my mother's effusion. No one and nothing has replaced it. Nevertheless, I've navigated my last decades fueled by the reserves of both her ebullience and my father's early confidence in me. When I want to impress him now, I text him something his grandchildren have accomplished, like "Developmental Milestone Alert: Augustus now takes responsibility for his own mucus!"

Dad still speaks to me through books. He sent a couple to our first and only baby shower, books with a very clear message.

Our baby shower was a "book shower." David and his husband, Mark, offered to throw us a party and suggested this theme, knowing my aversion to traditional baby showers. I'm not so into the all-lady guest lists and the "cakes" made out of diapers. I hate diaper cakes. I hate them because anything that looks like a tiered white cake should be delicious and not made of something to absorb human waste. And I didn't want to do that thing where you murder the momentum by making folks sit in a circle while you open every single present and hold up each onesie and stick out your bottom lip to make that faux sad look that says, "Y'ALL. This is so ADORABLE it's actually making me DIE."

But the book shower idea—that changed everything. Because a pregnant approval junkie wants to have a baby shower that is unique and also gay. No one appreciates how hard it is to make a baby more than men who love men. My brother and brother-in-law showered us in a Chelsea loft. This party was basically a bevy of beautiful boys bearing books like *The Paper Bag Princess*. At this shower, it was raining men <u>and</u> books, two of my favorite things. It looked like a Dewey Decimal–themed tea dance on a gay cruise.

My father sent literary emissaries to the shower for "AC," as he sometimes calls our boy: *Moby Dick* and *Portrait of the Artist as a Young Man*. They are beautiful hardbound editions with leather covers. He dedicated the Melville with, "Augustus—Bon Voyage!" And the Joyce, "Augustus—Become your own work of art." Granted, I don't think the kid will be reading those soon—at least not until I start prepping him for kindergarten interviews. But I know why my dad sent those books to his preborn grandson and wrote those words. He's saying something by gifting his two favorite pieces of literature, rather than some Dr. Seuss. What he's saying is that I'm an old mom, which means my dad is an even older grandfather, which means he may not be alive when his grandson cracks the classics. After he's gone, my father wants to be there somehow for Augustus.

Those books sit on the kids' bookshelf, unopened. I pray my dad will be around when Augustus reads them. But if he's not, which is not unlikely, I hope that my father's grandson will appreciate the pointy handwriting of the inscription. I hope the boy, probably by then a young man, will feel the confidence that his grandfather had in him, that he would grow to appreciate the legacy of words with their ready-to-be-unearthed meanings.

Now my father's daughter has written a book of her own. Now that I'm a grown woman, I'll be just fine if he's more surprised than impressed.

My Husband's Dog Is Not My Kids' Brother

This is how it happens.

We are walking down the street as a family—at least one of us is wearing a kid, and John has his dog on a leash. A stranger walking toward us takes notice and smiles our way.

"What a beauty! So sweet!" the stranger coos.

I think the stranger has excellent taste. Until I notice s/he is talking about Korbin the dog and not a human-child. S/he bends down to continue the conversation with the animal.

"Are you a gooooood big brother? I bet you aaaaaa-rrrrrre . . . !"

My husband smiles. He and the stranger are now instantly familiar, because they are "Dog People." They talk about breeds and "rescues" and unconditional love. I blink. I stare. I cry (in my head), *MY HUSBAND'S DOG IS NOT MY KIDS' BROTHER*.

The main reason that my husband's dog is not my kids' brother is that my children are *Homo sapiens* with opposable thumbs, and the dog is a *Canis lupus* who eats his own vomit. Korbin was born covered in fur; Augustus and Minerva were born covered with vernix and meconium, respectively. Other noteworthy differences:

- Dogs smell. If it rains on my children, their scent does not induce gagging.
- Dogs don't talk. Yes, they communicate, but they do not form words to ask interesting questions like, "Do dinosaurs have nipples?"
- While it is true that, like dogs, babies need their poop cleaned up, this only lasts about two years. Even if I throw Dog People a bone and calculate poop in dog years, that's like fourteen years of dealing with my children's ordure versus approximately eighty-four years of putting a plastic bag over your hand and wrapping it around soft, warm dog shit.

Let me get this over with: I think animals are great, dogs in particular. Dogs bring many people joy. A dog can lower its owner's blood pressure. (Since I'm not Korbin's owner, he raises <u>my</u> blood pressure, especially when he barks at anyone he doesn't like and everyone he does like.) And reportedly, all the disgusting dander and fur that constantly accumulates in my home is good for the children's immune systems. Dogs can sniff out cancer! A dog dialed 911!!

So dogs are wonderful creatures. I would think yours is adorable. I just don't want one. Besides the fact that, scientifically speaking, their mouths are NOT cleaner than humans', here are a few reasons why:

- I like privacy. You're never alone when you have a dog. At least kids go to school for part of the day. Dogs are always around. If you forget they are around, they will remind you or your nose.

- Name one thing convenient about having a dog. Dogs are a significant responsibility if you are a decent owner and offer them food, exercise, and grooming. Small children require even more caretaking, but all your efforts pay off eventually. Not so with dogs. Dogs will never help you match socks out of the dryer or thank you in their valedictory remarks or announce that they just made a heart-shaped poop because they "love you so much."

- Your husband takes his dog out every morning while you deal with children by yourself—kids who resist your a.m. administration of probiotic powder until it looks like you've all gone on a coke binge.

- Your husband takes the dog out for the nighttime walk, pipe in hand, instead of spending time with you, watching the DVR backlog of *Downton Abbey*, during the precious forty-five minutes between both children down and your bedtime.

- Hairy dog penises I didn't ask to see.

Oh, how I tried to want one, or at least want someone else's. When I met John, he had two dogs—Louisiana Catahoula leopard dogs, to be exact. Korbin and Maggie (RIP). I loved John, so I really tried to love his dogs. That didn't work, so I tried to like them. I settled for tolerating their hair all over my everything and accepting the fact that while I was in John's bed, they were allowed to sleep on John's bed. They were fine dogs, mostly annoying insofar as their existence meant that John could never, ever stay at my apartment and I always, always had to pack up and spend the weekend at John, Korbin, and Maggie's apartment. I would pet them and talk to them and go on walks with John and the Catahoulas. One time, when John was sick in bed, I became the world's best girlfriend by offering to take ancient Maggie out and pick up her business. She ran a loose business, so I almost threw up. Then I was almost run over, because she let it go in the middle of the street, and the taxi drivers were not happy waiting for me to scoop up crap that technically belonged to my boyfriend.

I learned something about John's dogs after we were married and moved into a new apartment together. I learned that I don't want dogs and dog smells and dog noises in my own home. It was too late. We were married, and John came with the dogs, like shedding, incontinent stepchildren.

I think John thought he married, not a dog lover, but at least a dog *liker*. Even though I didn't mean to, he may feel like I pulled a mate and switch.

In the past few years, there have been a few manifestos written by women who have happily decided to be child-free and want society not to stigmatize them. I support those well-rested ladies with innie belly buttons. But if you mention you don't want a pet, you get pilloried. If you are not a Pet Person, you are a Bad Person.

Take a recent conversation with Juan, the daily dog walker. The kids call him Uncle Juan, but say it like, "Un Kwon," probably making Juan the only Ecuadorian dog walker to have a Korean name. Un Kwon looks remarkably like Salvador Dali. Un Kwon is an agent of chaos. He tosses stuff for the dog to fetch in the apartment, waking up napping children. He encourages them to throw dinner on the floor for the dog. Un Kwon takes avocado meant for Augustus's mouth and massages it into my son's hair, sculpting a food mohawk. And we chat like this on the topic of my not enjoying a dog in our apartment:

UN KWON: I like jew becoz I know jew, but if I deedn't know jew, I wouldn't like jew.

ME: What about people who don't like children, do you like them?

UN KWON: I hab no probleem wi dat.

ME: You have no problem when people don't like little babies. Small humans.

UN KWON: Ees fine wi me. Buh how can a pairson not like dugs?

ME: I like dogs fine, dogs are great, I just don't want one.

UN KWON: Jew crazy. Korbie lufs jew.

ME: No he doesn't, Juan. I feed Korbie, that's all. He knows which side of his bone is buttered.

That Un Kwon barely likes me shouldn't surprise me. I once did a commentary for *Sunday Morning*, the world's most folksy TV show, called "I Am Not a Pet Person." My basic point was that although, yes, I loved our French poodle

Jacques Le Strap as a child, I don't want a pet now. So please don't judge me as Cruella de Vil, and I'll try not to judge <u>you</u> as crazy when you French kiss your pet or dress your "baby" up in people clothes or throw a "barkmitzvah."

Sunday Morning airs on Sunday mornings. The amount of rabid comments I received on the Christian Sabbath stunned me. Granted, they were not of the same creative pornographic ilk as the hate I've gotten from Fox News viewers. When it comes to which audience spews more vitriol, it's a question of quality versus quantity.

First, let's take quality. Here's some constructive criticism my Fox appearances have earned:

> *you really don't have much of a sense of humor for a fat asses skank*
>
> *Robert S.*

> *And you're a complete tool because?????*
>
> *Jay N Vanessa*

> *You have a Stupid airline SLUT!!!!appearance*
> *You cow like creature, very disgusting . . . Smelly like. You slutty bitch!!! Fondest Regards*
>
> *Steve B.*

> *You know, you are, without a doubt, the most vile human I have ever seen on TV. Why don't you go back to O Magazine with Oprah, and the pigs on The View. . . . you would fit right in.*
>
> *Ms. Barbara W.*

I don't know if you have kids.. . . . but I'm sure if you do. . . . when they were born they must have smelled like fish. You probably aborted your pregnancies. Have a great life funny girl BTW.. . . . getting a late start attempting to be in show biz aren't you?

Respectfully,

Kim

You should stick to failed comedy attempts (aka grade school sarcasm) and leave the thinking to men. Play to your strengths. Then people won't keep mistaking you for a fire hydrant. And you'll stay much drier.

manhood101

And now for quantity. My "I Am Not a Pet Person" commentary delivered hundreds of responses. Most of them said that it's clear I've never been unconditionally loved; one said I needed to get some sun.

Then there was Pam.

I would like to give Faith a cigarette to calm her down after her "I don't want pets" segment on CBS Sunday Morning. In fact, I'll be happy to give her a case of cigarette's.

My boyfriend would be perfect for you, he doesn't like pets either, nor does he like women who own dogs. You're both skinny and uptight, find disgust in everything that you do not produce. Others see your disgust, they are just too kind (a trait learned from pets) to tell you about your scrawny, disgusting persona you cherish and force onto others.

I think there are rescue agencies for people like Faith and

my boyfriend, it's called the Russian Space program, join it,
the planet will be better off without you.

Sincerely
-Pam

If she hadn't mentioned the dogs, I totally would've pegged Pam as a Cat Lady. I e-mailed her back, told her I was marrying a man with two dogs, and thanked her for thinking I was skinny. She wrote me back saying maybe I'm not as bad as she'd thought, but her boyfriend is the worst.

The sheer volume of the Pet Person comments hit me hard. So many people took the time to express their disapproval of me on a show I care about. A sweet show I used to watch as a child, over pancakes with my family, before church. My friend Mo Rocca* is a correspondent on the show, and one day he called me out of the blue to suggest I write a couple of commentaries he could show to the executive producer, Rand Morrison. I immediately wrote four samples and met with Rand. I tried to remain cool as I talked to the architect behind what's pretty much *the greatest show in the history of television*. Rand gave me a shot, then gave me more and more shots. But all those shots did not inoculate me against the virulent comment bath in which my Pet Person piece dunked me. I read every single one, feeling

---

* This was a fairy godfather gesture of generosity on Mo's part that changed my life. Mo is a phenomenal gift giver. At our baby book shower, he gifted our unborn son with a collection of vintage *TV Guides* from the '70s. My favorite shows a gauzy Suzanne Somers in what appears to be a flowered beekeeper's hat with the caption, "I Want It All." Tucked inside, we found a card: "Dearest Augustus, Your parents are busy right now. If you're bored, change the channel. Love, Mo."

sicker and sicker but unable to stop. It was like bingeing but without the temporary thrill of trans fats.

But _where_ this all took place is key. I pored over these comments while sitting by the fire in the lobby of a monastery-turned-hotel in Prague. It was a cold, clear April night. John had taken me to Europe for my fortieth birthday. He was outside stargazing, exhaling his pipe tobacco. I was inside, inhaling others' vitriol.

John found me in the lobby, robbing Eastern Europe of its Wi-Fi. He was a bit breathless, and I was teary. He wanted to show me the sky, but first he asked me what was wrong.

"My pet person commentary aired, and everyone hates me! They're so mean! They think I'm ugly and stupid and horrible! I was just being funny! I even said I like animals!"

John braced my shoulders.

"Baby. Why do you read that stuff? Think about it: what kind of people take the time to write shit online? They're crazy, especially pet people."

"But you love dogs _and_ you love me!" I sniffled.

"Yes. And I don't dress my dogs up like Abraham Lincoln or push them in strollers in Central Park. They're crazy. But listen. Just stop. Why do you do this to yourself? Just don't read it. Don't let them enroll you in their energy. Look where we are!"

John says things like "enroll you in their energy," even though he doesn't do yoga.

Then he led me outside to look at the stars to remind me we were literally half a world away from all that didn't matter and gave me a lovely kiss that tasted gross.

I'd wanted the CBS audience to embrace me. I'd wanted

the executive producers to think I was a fan fave. I didn't need people to agree with me; I just wanted them to like me. I was STUPID, the commenters were right about that. Because you can't have it all. In fact, if you're a woman, and you try to win approval by expressing your opinion, you're probably going to succeed 30 percent of the time. The other 70 percent of the time, you're fielding questions about the effluvium of your birth canal.

Early on, I confess it was fun to discover a thread in a chat room devoted to whether or not I should get bangs. But that frisson of self-importance quickly deteriorated because people can be downright mean. Reading things about myself is, at some level, a self-excoriating exercise in feeling important. I try not to do it anymore. My father occasionally calls to tell me I should ignore all the horrible comments I haven't read. It's best just to tell myself, quietly, *WHEN U READ THESE COMMENT'S YOUR LETTING UR EGO HAVE IT'S WAY!!!**

I'm now convinced that if I want a loyal audience for my opinions, I should probably get my own dog.

---

* Sic, sic, sic. It's totally sic.

Breastfeeding Sucks

Nobody told me that breastfeeding would leave me with blood running down my face.

You sit in twilight, in a position you've assumed hundreds of times before. Your baby touches you like a lover—there's no other way to put it, sorry to be weird. But you know each other—you know every curve of her face; she knows every curve of your milk delivery system. She grazes you with her hands, she clasps her chubby little fingers around your wrist, proprietary. With her other hand she languidly fiddles with your wedding ring. Then gently entwines her fingers with yours. No one else will ever experience this moment with this child except you. Her hand reaches for your face, and she shoves her fingers straight up both of your nostrils. You learn that a baby finger is exactly nostril-size, and you learn that you need to clip her fingernails. As you begin to bleed from the lacerations, you remove her fingers, and she decides they should land in your mouth. She laughs as she scrapes your gums with the thoroughness of a Virgo periodontist.

This has happened on multiple occasions.

I'm going to tell you something else no one told me about breastfeeding, something very important. But first let's review the things they *did* tell me. And by "they," I mean everyone from girlfriends to strangers. Everyone has a thought. A cleaning lady once helpfully pointed out, upon seeing me wearing wedges soon after giving birth, "The heel is bad for the milk."

My mother-in-law, who chose not to express milk, was quick to express skepticism of "those lactation people" whom I enlisted to help me. I did receive overt approbation from the French family who lives directly upstairs from us with their two feral youngsters. One afternoon as they were lunching on the public terrace that abuts our living room window, I walked by the window topless, save for a tiny baby covering one breast. The whole family gave me raucous thumbs-up. However, they are French, so I think they were mocking me.

Here are the things I was told about breastfeeding.

It's Miraculous

First and foremost, are we all clear on how this works? Oh no big D, except that YOUR BODY TAKES YOUR BLOOD AND TURNS IT INTO MILK. I mean, really stop and think about that. That's some Jesus-like shit right there. Sure, Jesus could turn water into wine, and wine has resveratrol. But ladies can turn blood into milk, and milk has natural galacto-oligosaccharides, which is not a word I made up. Someone named God or Darwin, I guess, created this system, and it's how the human race solely survived until the first cavewoman with sore nipples grunted "Screw this" and invented formula.

Yes, breast milk is barely believably amazing. It's reliably, freshly available; it's just the right temperature; it has fatty acids and unicorn DNA to turn your babies into polyglot physicists. Research has shown that breastfed children possess higher IQs than formula kids. Now I don't know if this is really true, because my older child survived almost entirely on formula and, like all parents, I suspect my own child is a genius. But I do know that my entirely breastfed younger child has sucked the intelligence out of me. For the past year, I've called elephants "umbrellas" and hailed downtown taxis to take me uptown.

It's Healthy

Nothing's healthier for your baby than your breast milk. Unless you're my son. After ten weeks of life, surviving only on what I'd served on tap, my son had dropped off the growth chart. It wasn't that I didn't have enough milk—don't mean to brag, but I'm what's known as "an overproducer." No, my baby suffered a severe milk-soy protein allergy that caused blood to streak his diapers and him to scream anytime I put him on me, so our pediatrician prescribed a sci-fi-sounding "elemental medical food for infants who cannot tolerate intact or hydrolyzed protein." This formula smelled like chlorine. I had to quit breastfeeding him cold turkey. Then I spent months on a strict elimination diet so I didn't ingest anything that might remotely upset his system. I was one of those freaks who had to tell waiters that not a bit of butter could touch her food, probably ensuring that a lot of their saliva touched my food. I pumped and dumped for weeks to make sure my milk was "clean," and by that time, Augustus refused to take my breast. So I joylessly pumped around the clock so I could add breast milk to his bottles. Even my lactation consultant Rhona told me I'd gone above and beyond. Rhona is the hip, cool Jewish grandmother from Yonkers you want for your children. I was sitting in the dark at our dining table on the phone with her. My scrawny baby was sleeping, and my husband was once again working late. From my seat, I could see the skyline. I felt completely alone in a city full of mothers with chunky babies. Rhona said, "You've done more than anyone could humanly expect. It's okay to give up, Faith."

Did I stop pumping? Well, of course not. I pumped because I felt like it was something I could do to help a situation over which I had no control. I pumped because I was his mother and felt like I'd failed him in some primal way—*I can't feed my baby*.

So when I finally had another baby, I wanted her to suck it up.

It's Convenient

Breastfeeding is superconvenient, because you don't have to mix formula, put it in bottles, and warm it up. This is entirely true for the father and the nonlactating lesbian mother.

However, if you are the milk lady, it really comes down to your definition of convenient: Do you think it's convenient to pour some powder in water and shake up a bottle? Or do you find it easier to engage in public nudity, quite possibly on a cold day or on a flight seated next to a Hasidic Jew who doesn't even want your elbow to touch his? Perhaps you do find it convenient to be constantly on call so that, five minutes after you sneak out of your home to have one single half hour to yourself, taking with you your gym bag and your breasts, you receive a text composed with the nanny's signature pith: "he up." Also, maybe instead of knowing how many ounces your child is consuming by looking at a bottle, you find it handier to lift your breast and then your baby up and down to see if one feels lighter and the other heavier.

Pumping was invented (a) to make breastfeeding convenient and (b) as a humiliation device. One time I sat down on the airplane toilet, ready, as usual, to pump while traveling and realized I'd forgotten to pack the breast shields. Without shields, there was no flow, <u>and</u> I couldn't fight crime. I tried to use my hands to squeeze out an ounce, but it felt like a one-woman S&M show. I missed the equivalent of two feedings and arrived engorged at my hotel to find the concierge had mistakenly delivered me a manual pump rather than the parts I needed. I was in town to make jokes on NPR, but all I could do was cry while I sat on the hotel bed half naked, trying to extract a few ounces with the rickety hand pump.

I'm never embarrassed about pumping, but I do find the loud farting noises the pump makes when I adjust my breasts distasteful. When my son hears this, he announces, "Mommy has gas." I always want to emerge from the public restroom stall and let everyone know it wasn't me, it was my boobs. And no matter how much discretion I seek by choosing a stall at the end of the row, the metronomic whir of the pump gives me away like the beating of Poe's telltale heart.

The pump is supposed to untether you, make you a gal

on the move, a lactating Jean Naté. Look at you, you're a working woman <u>and</u> a mama! What the pump really does is weigh you down, along with the ice pack you have to take with you to keep your fluids fresh. Because of the nature of what I do, "pumping at work" has found me pumping in a wing of the CDC with a security guard standing by and in waders on an oyster farm. Let's not factor the convenience of how long it takes the TSA to test fifteen bottles individually after a two-and-a-half-day business trip. I mean. If I were a suicide bomber, you'd better believe I would not have spent my last sixty hours on earth hooked up to a Medela Pump In Style.

It's Painful

I understand breastfeeding hurts some people. Their nipples crack or bleed. Not mine. I have pioneer woman nipples. A saleswoman at the Upper Breastside (our neighborhood "milk bar," whose slogan is "You bring your breasts, we've got the rest!") watched in awe as I tested out a hospital-grade pump and turned it up to the maximum suckage. "Wow," she whispered, eyes wide. "Most women can't handle that." This from a gal named Bianca who's seen a lot of nipples pulled in and out of flanges. I asked her if she had a stronger model. My nipples can go to eleven.

I can take breastfeeding when it sucks, but I can't take it when it bites.

Minerva went through two spells of biting me. Each lasted over a week. She thought it was really funny. I thought it was really obnoxious. I also started to live in fear. She and I were alone on her first Valentine's Day, and my little lover spent the day biting the crap out of me. I've had to fill a box with objects to distract her so she doesn't chomp. These objects, which I call Weapons of Mass Distraction, include but are not limited to: an iPhone charger, a Lord of the Teething Ring necklace, an expired Amex card, and a hippo keychain.

While she's on me, I hand them to her, one by one, for her to scrutinize, rotate, and then listlessly fling over her shoulder as if she's Cleopatra.

It's Soothing

There was a night, around when Minerva turned a year old, when she was sick. She kept uncharacteristically waking up—first mewing, then crying, clearly in discomfort. All I knew to do, after dosing her with Motrin and trying to cradle her, was to put her on my breast. She didn't want her father. But I was so, so exhausted. I was frustrated that I was the only thing that could soothe her—and not even entirely, at that. I was giving her my body. I couldn't give her more. It was like I was Jesus or something. But Jesus never had to worry about having his nipple severed while he sacrificed himself. I sat there in the dark, in what should have been this beautiful moment of motherhood, resenting the whole setup, asking God why She ever even bothered to give men nipples.

It's Bonding

Breastfeeding Minerva has made me belong to her in a way I've never belonged to anyone before.

Sometimes I want to consume her as much as she consumes me, which is to say I can't get enough of kissing her, smelling her, smushing her cheeks in my lips. Our three to sixteen daily feeding sessions have separated me from my husband and from my son. She and I disappear into the breastfeeding corner, and I close the door behind us. When Augustus asks to sit on my lap or for me to read him a book or pick him up, I have to say, "I will, honey, as soon as I'm done with your sister." I register the flash of pain on his face as he's reminded, yet again, he's been knocked down in the pecking order. I feel awful that I have to triage one baby before another.

What this has also meant is that my day—"my" day, the moments that I spent either happily or guiltily away from my child, especially during her first six months—was constantly interrupted. Breastfeeding forced me to quit whatever else I was doing all day long and sit quietly with my newborn, who has become almost a little girl, literally under my eyes. For all the times it felt like a chore and for all the times I missed wearing turtlenecks, I was also depleting my potential future regret account. When I think back on this time, I won't remember whatever it was I was doing that got interrupted, but I will remember that I stopped, held my daughter in the purple glider, and looked down on her fuzzy head and perfect eyelashes.*

I never had to make a decision about weaning Augustus, because my fertility doctor told me to stop pumping once I started IVF drugs. It wasn't a tough choice between

---

* Sometimes I would look at my iPhone and google *How much kate middleton gain pregnant*

giving my son more milk or a sibling. I was relieved to stop
because I "had" to. I remember sitting in a hot bath about
a week after my last pumping session and barely touching
my nipple, just to see what would happen. Milk immediately emerged. I was overwhelmed with melancholy that I
hadn't known was still there—like the breast milk, sadness
had been suppressed but not evaporated. Those drops were a
manifestation of the life force that had improbably made my
son, and I was shutting it down (prematurely?) in a gamble
to make another baby.

Now I'm a little embarrassed that I'm breastfeeding Minerva well into her second year. I never thought I'd be one
of those women who made it past six months. I didn't give
birth to her at home in a pool. I didn't make a smoothie out
of my placenta. I don't sleep with her. But here I am, still
breastfeeding her three times a day. Here she is, at an age
when she actually says to me, "All done." I think I speak
for many of us when I say that's creepy. I'm still doing it
not because I love it or because of how much I love her; I'm
doing it because I'm not sure how to be her mother without
it. I guess that means I'm afraid to lose that connection even
though I want to be liberated from it.

I need to shut it down before the orthodontist pries my
teenaged daughter and her pitiful overbite off me. I want my
body back. I don't have anything interesting to do with it
once I get it back, but I'd like it back. It will be nice to start
drinking again during the day.

When I first wrote this chapter, it ended rather poeti-
cally. Minerva was six months old at the time, and I could
only conclude elliptically.

This is what I wrote:

So I do not want to stop. Or, more truly, I do not want her to stop. She is my last. I do not want my baby to stop being a baby yet. I do not want her to stop needing me and only me so fundamentally. I do not want her to stop opening her mouth eagerly as soon as I pull out my breast or making satisfied, quiet swallowing sounds while her hands try to yank my hair out of my scalp. I do not want to stop looking down at her delighted smile when she pops off and remembers Mommy's the vending machine. I do not want to cease being her source of energy. I do not want to get old. I do not want to dry up. I do not want things to end. We are a dyad I don't want to die.

That was true then, if mawkish. But now she's not a baby. She's a toddler, and she's walking away from me, just as she's supposed to.

So the real news, the thing that no one ever tells you about breastfeeding is this: it's both miraculous and brutal. It's both at the same time, and that's why it sucks so damn hard. Breastfeeding is exactly like motherhood—relentless and rewarding, depleting and renewing, universal and intimate, isolating and bonding, merciless and sweet, seemingly ceaseless but painfully fleeting.

For all these reasons breastfeeding sucks. And, for now, for just a little bit longer, will keep on sucking.

"All done."

A Stamp of Approval for My Daughter

Dear Minerva,

You already have my approval.

I hope I'll have yours.

I'm dedicating this chapter to you and not your brother, because, by the time you read this, I'm pretty sure the world won't have changed much. I'm pretty sure there will still be a million more ways for a woman to gain or lose approval than a man. If your brother identifies as a girl, then we'll all have lots to talk about and some clothes to share, but for now I think I have more to offer you by way of advice.

An improv expert once told me there are two different kinds of improvisers: floaters and scrappers. People always seem to envy the floaters, their unsavory name notwithstanding. Floaters don't worry about whether they'll be funny; they don't plan how a scene is going to go. They completely trust themselves, or maybe they're a little lazy.

Floaters float. I don't love floating, because I can't see what's under me. I've always been a scrapper. Planning (albeit futile in improv), practicing, trying, and trying again. In improv and in life, though, it's served me well. Still, I'm starting to float more, resting on the tide of my experience. I hope you will be both a scrapper and a floater. Maybe a scroater. No, that sounds gross. Be a flapper.

Seeking approval has not undone me. It's done me; it's dinged me; it's built me. I want the same for you. At this point in your life, I clap for you when you do something like eat corn. I anticipate the days when I applaud you for things like devouring books or gobbling up attention for—I don't know; you choose—poetry slamming or parkour or chocolate robotics competitions. (As of this writing, "chocolate robotics competitions" are something I just made up, but I hope they will exist by the time you're in high school, and you'll be the national champ and allow me to eat your failed inventions.)

So. A shortlist from your mother who doesn't always know best but has learned a lot . . .

- Coco Chanel: "Before you leave the house, look in the mirror and remove one accessory." Your mother: "Before you leave the apartment, look in the mirror and remove your Breathe Right Nasal Strip."
- There are many second chances to make a first impression, because people forget. They forget you! This is good news! Or they just don't remember how bad you might have bit it!
- Dry shampoo makes life 33 percent easier.

- Don't sleep with people just to prove you can. That's not exactly sticking it to the Man.
- Focus on being beautiful if you want to get something from people. Focus on being smart and/or funny if you want to give something to people.
- It's okay to get angry at people who deserve it.
- Don't hold on to the treadmill. This is both an earnest workout tip and a life lesson. Who are these people who get on the treadmill and then clutch it while they walk uphill, half-assed? Let go and trust yourself that you can go harder. If the incline feels too steep, then slow yourself down, even as you march uphill. You can't speed past the arduous slogs in life. You need to summon all your energy if you want results. (The other thing about hanging on to the treadmill is that it's very germy.)
- Don't change yourself for someone else. Change yourself for you, as often as needed . . . it's how you discover who you are.
- Ignore people who talk about "safety schools" and "back-up plans." Be safe in traffic and sex but not in life goals.
- There is no downside to:
  - Making good grades
  - Doing the extra credit
  - Not doing drugs
  - Praying
  - Asking questions, except "Does this make me look fat?" and "Do you love me?"
  - Taking the stairs

- Learning people's names
- Writing thank-you notes
- There's probably a downside to consuming artificial sweetener, but this is a do as I say and not as I do bullet point
- Marry a mensch who's generous enough to think he's lucky.
- Don't miss out on the kind of heartbreaks and disappointments that propel you. (I know I'm supposed to want you to have a better life than I have, even though I pretty much love my life, despite the fact that you may have noticed we don't have a washer/dryer in our home. I pray you have your own washer/dryer as you approach middle age.) Anyway, my point is, the things you think you've lost, like jobs and loves and babies, either come back around or leave a fertile wake.

I hope that you'll care just enough about the approval of others that you will always try your hardest, even if it's to flout or flummox your detractors. Or, better yet, to win laughter from your supporters.

I hope you'll care a lot about winning your own approval—enough to stretch, appreciate, and occasionally embarrass yourself.

And this may be my most impossible wish: I hope you'll love yourself as much as I love you.

Acknowledgments

My friend Don says that if you get to the end of your story, and you're the hero, you told it wrong. We've come to the end. These are my heroes.

To my editor, Suzanne O'Neill, I hope you permanently fall into the arms of someone who often tells you what I'm about to: You're always right. You made me dig so deep that I wrote most of this book in China. Thank you for having all that—there's no other way to say it—*faith* in me.

Fairy godmothers exist. Mine was Rachel Klayman, who generously read my idea for a book, met me for lunch on a rainy day, and offered to send my "stuff" to Suzanne O'Neill and Daniel Greenberg. Rachel, *thank you* is not enough for being my Patient Zero, responsible for spreading my words. (And thank you, David Edelstein, for your good taste in women.)

Daniel Greenberg, besides my husband, you are the best set-up of my life. A massive *grazie* for the patience and therapy and for saving me from some of my own jokes. I have no idea if other agents are as dedicated, smart, and caring as you, and I intend never to find out.

Thanks to the beautifully supportive team at Crown—Molly Stern, Tammy Blake, Julie Cepler, Matt Inman, Trish Boczkowski, Courtney Snyder, Annsley Rosner, Gianna Antolos, Jenni Zellner, Julia Elliott, Matthew Martin, Kelsey Lawrence, and Tina "Blue Light" Constable. Also to Tim Wojcik at LGR and Mauro DiPreta.

Joanne Napolitano will tell me to shut up while I thank her, but I won't. Thank you for being my platonic wife, my tireless reader, my Creamsicle Chew dealer, and for reminding me of MWS10. Let's not fight about who loves whom more.

Seth Godin, I know you don't need public gratitude, but you just have to sit there and accept it. You've taken so much of my chit. Every syllable of wisdom you shared with me has been true and invaluable. The problem with you, Seth, is I can never repay you, because you don't want me to. I can tell you had a great mom.

Jancee Dunn, thank you to infinity, for being there always, a text or e-mail or lunch away. Thank you for being the most charitable writer and friend. Thank you for making me snort with laughter when I needed it and for getting empathetically stressed for me and stuffing Pirate's Booty in your mouth.

Henriette Lazaridis, from Dunster House to Old John's, thank you for being first a tutor, then a mentor, now a dear friend. Please close read me forever.

I'm grateful to friends who read versions of this along the way and kept me (arguably) from totally embarrassing myself: Lindsay Sturman, Mario Correa, J. J. Miller.

Thank you to my friends who witnessed the rock bottom of my junkiness and never looked away—April Audia,

Julie Ann Lowery, Kathleen McMartin. You Three Graces offered me hands to get up. Nell Benjamin and Vonnie Murad, you kept checking in on me. Amy James and Rachel Spears, you've always approved, for some crazy reason, and I love you for it.

Dr. Maureen Moomjy, you've given me so much to write about and some of the most insightful notes ever, especially for someone who also has to focus on creating humans. Elanna Posner and Doctors Gabrielle Francis and Ilana Brownstein helped deliver these stories.

Sharon Schuster, for that prayer and all the images that remind me what's important.

Mamie Healey, I feel like a *macher* that I get to thank you for your early-and-always support.

Manfred Kuhnert, without you there is no book. Thank you for encouraging me to be "Nakedly Human Publicly."

Thank you to Adam Nettler at CAA for telling me I had to write a book and to Cait Hoyt for suggesting I write *this* book. Thank you to Michelle Howry for being the first person to suggest I could write a book (except for that psychic named Theo, pronounced "TAY-oh," back in 1998).

Brian Fenwick and Jo Honig made sure I had a room of one's own. Brad Mislow and Julie Abes were Spartan fact-checkers.

Thank you, Rand Morrison, for your support and patience.

Peter Sagal, kudos for your great idea.

Heartfelt gratitude to the people who helped love and care for my kids while I was writing: Gabrielle Salie, Lorei Salie, Isabelle Salie, Robert Lee, Angela South, Natalie Nevares, Suzy Giordano, Melody Swaby, Marci Guarriello,

Deb Malkoff, Abby Gail Boyd, Victoria Oliver, Joelle Ganzoni. It takes a village to raise a book.

Sincere thanks to everyone who appears in this book, even if I changed your name, even if you'll never read this, or will greatly disapprove of it. You were all part of this story. As Rascal Flatts sings, "Others who broke my heart, they were like Northern stars / Pointing me on my way. . . ." Thank you, Faith Salie, for quoting Rascal Flatts. You're welcome.

To my family—Dad, Doug, David, Mark, Lorei, Rita—thank you for letting me write about you, no questions asked. And especially to my father, whom I can never thank enough for gifting me a life worth writing about.

Thank you to my children, Augustus Cosimo and Minerva Gail Salie-Semel, who were tiny babies when I started this book, and who bloomed into sweet, happy people as I wrote it. You gave me the motivation to power through it, so I could finish and go play with you.

To my husband, John Semel, beside whom I'm literally sitting in the Roman Forum, writing these words on my laptop while you take a conference call, my deepest thanks for this journey. It started somewhat late, but we've made up for lost time. Now may we amble, hand in hand, through the rest of our lives.

And last but not least, to the one who approved of me first and always, thank you, Mom.

FAITH SALIE is an Emmy-winning contributor to *CBS News Sunday Morning* and a panelist on NPR's *Wait Wait . . . Don't Tell Me!* She also hosts the PBS show *Science Goes to the Movies*. As a commentator on politics and pop culture, she's been interviewed by the likes of Oprah Winfrey, Bill O'Reilly, and Anderson Cooper. As a television and public radio host, she herself has interviewed newsmakers from Lorne Michaels to President Carter to Robert Redford, who invited her to call him "Bob." Faith attended Oxford University on a Rhodes Scholarship, and while her fellow scholars went on to become governors and mayors, she landed on a *Star Trek* collectible trading card worth hundreds of cents. She lives in New York City with her husband, two children, and her husband's dog.

APPROVAL JUNKIE
EXTRA LIBRIS

ESSAYS,
READER'S GUIDES,
AND MORE

A New Chapter

Do your work, then step back. The only
path to serenity.

—*Lao Tzu*

After this book was published, the Barnes & Noble in
my neighborhood put a massive blow-up of its cover
in their front window. For a while they also exhibited
a large photo of me, sassily attempting to jut my hip
out in a dress no one would ever guess I purchased
at Target during the first Obama administration.
The first few times I saw this display, it was terrifi-
cally exciting—a larger-than-life advertisement for
a dream realized. After a successful event there—
during which Mo Rocca became the only person on
my entire book tour to ask me about Matt Damon's
privates—the store kept my cover on display. For
months, friends would text me: "omg!!!your book in
B&N window!!!" Driving by the store in taxis, my
kids eventually took to remarking, "There's Mommy's book!" as if it were just another game of I Spy.

After a few months, my face was no longer in the

window and my book was relocated from the front of the store by the Godiva chocolates to a new home on the second floor, in Actor Biographies, near the unauthorized Adam Sandler story.

When I mentioned this to my husband—a man who is not at all effusive but constantly reveals himself to be constant—he emerged as the world's best partner. As he'd done every time I'd expressed any anxiety surrounding the publication of my book, John patiently reminded me, "Remember why you wrote it."

"I know, I know," I said, dismissively. "I wanted to tell my story." I recited this in monotone to demonstrate that telling my story seemed, at the moment, to mean very little.

"And you did!" John said.

"But I want more people to *read* it!" I responded.

(I should note here that people *were* reading it. People have read it. People do read it, and I thank you right now. But approval junkiness can be a terrible friend—it may enable you to throw yourself a celebration, but right after you clink champagne glasses, it can crinkle its nose and sniff, "Oh, this is just Prosecco?")

"Baby," he said. (Fittingly.) "You did it. It's done. You had a dream to write a book, and you achieved it. Do you know how few people can say that? The rest is just numbers and luck, and Oprah picking your book." (Are you there, Oprah? It's me, Faith.)

John sat me down and blinked deliberately, because his eyes started to well up. He added, "And you know what else your book did? It gave us this experience. I'm getting a chance to watch you live your dream. I know it doesn't always feel like you are, but you are. And I get to be proud of you." Now that kind of compliment beats the shit out of "The way you look in those jeans makes me want to jump you, consensually" or any of the 207 other compliments I've tried, unsuccessfully, to tease out of him.

But while his patient support kept me afloat, it didn't douse my ambitions. Putting a book out in the world was new territory for me. Most of what I do professionally is in the public arena. I know I've made a decent joke, because I hear an audience laugh. I can sense whether I've conducted a good interview, because I know what a true connection feels like (or sometimes the person simply says, "Thank you—that was so much fun."). Less publicly, I'm certain when I've pulled off, say, a 3-D excavator cake for my son's birthday, because it doesn't collapse, and also a gaggle of four-year-olds is running in circles fueled by FD&C Yellow No. 5. But my book . . . how could I know the answers to *Is this good? Is it funny? Is it meaningful?* I was too close to it for so long, and moreover, it's my own story—how could I judge it?

Of course, for any author, there's the question of whether you ought to read the reviews. Well, of course one reads one's reviews in magazines and newspapers. But it's the ones on Amazon and Goodreads that might give you pause. I did read them at first, assiduously checking for new reviews. Interestingly, I found it much easier to absorb the pointy blows of the one-star reviewers than the two- or three-star givers. (Four- and five-star givers: Coca-Cola cake is in the mail.) At the very least, I could tell myself that some of my one-star detractors had wanted a book that I simply hadn't written.

This book is vulgar and uninteresting. I don't understand why pulp fiction and trashy "romance" novels have such a wide readership, but they do.

I made it 22 pages into this novel and junked it (no pun intended). It was not humorous at all, though she's supposed to be a sort of comedian.

And this one-star reviewer offered perhaps the most emphatic review of *Approval Junkie*:

The worst piece of garbage I've ever purchased thru Amazon . . . what a total waste of money and my time! How in the world did this author find a publisher? I think I'll do some dumpster writing and have this publisher put a book out to the world!

But my lowest point wasn't available to the public. It came while relaxing on my brother's Florida porch on a blistering summer day explaining to my dad how I'd not wanted to put my son in any kind of day camp, because I'd hardly gotten to see my kids for the previous two summers while I was writing my book. "Oh?" my father said, feigning surprise, "And how did that work out for you?" This sarcasm was surely my dad's idea of a joke, and it was definitely as hilarious as Dr. Phil doing stand-up. The reason my father's words hurt so much was they echoed my darkest question: *Did writing this book matter?*

The weeks went by, pages turned, and my need to stargaze waned, allowing me to give this idea more and more thought. In quieter moments, I could really start to recall the answers to John's gentle entreaty:

Remember why you wrote it.

During the time I was writing all but this last chapter you hold in your hand, these were my answers:

I write because I finally believe I have something to say.

I want to make people laugh and maybe cry and maybe both, possibly even at the same time. Because, like Truvy says in *Steel Magnolias,* "Laughter through tears is my favorite emotion," and Truvy is right about everything.

I want to connect with—dare I say inspire— someone who has ever lost her mother or her marriage or a baby or a job or eyelashes . . . or herself.

I want to thank my husband, my brothers, my father.

To give my mom life.

To encourage someone who wants to become a mother.

To help someone learn to listen.

Because hardly anyone talks about miscarriages.

I write to defend these human needs—to be heard, understood, loved.

I want to connect with strangers in whom, mysteriously, I feel I can confide.

I write because I can't not. Even if it means using a double negative.

But now I know that there were more reasons, ones I could have barely imagined when I started writing these stories:

Because I got to walk into Barnes & Noble with both my father and my son on the day my book came out. My three-year-old informed the security man at the door that he was there to see his book, because, "Mommy dedicated it to me." And I stood by the center table in the store with *Approval Junkie* on display, holding my boy and standing by my dad . . . who might have been a little impressed.

Because I was invited to read this book before rooms of open-hearted people and hear them laugh and witness how my words traveled through the air and flitted across their faces as emotion.

I wrote so I could get a real-time tweet from someone named Charlotte on a bus in Cambridge, England, telling me that my story about my dad and the literature he and I shared is making her cry.

So that I could get a text from my dad that our story made him cry.

I got to thank my mistakes, which meant forgiving myself.

I got to recognize the faith my husband has in me. John never asked to read a word of my manuscript before it was published. (Even though I offered. Repeatedly.) He trusted me to do right by him and to tell my own story.

So I could wrestle with the challenge of crafting myself as a "character." This turned out be a gift, because it asks you to show yourself compassion.

I learned that writing offers a kind of time travel that unleashes your ghosts and forces you to dance with them until they reinter themselves.

So I could walk into the first book club I've ever attended and actually be the author they were discussing (!). I sat among Atlanta gals who were downing wine and red velvet cupcakes in a ratio that strongly favored the vino, and we got to "Truvy" it up. A woman named Jennifer confessed that, based on the title of my book, she had assumed it wasn't for her. Then she told me she'd lost her mom and thanked me in tears for sharing my grief. Jennifer's husband reportedly kept asking her why she was crying while reading a book that was supposed to be funny. A pastor named Katie said what I wrote about my mother's prayer for me became the focus of her church's prayer group. I was deeply honored. Neither of us brought up the hand job chapter.

So my friend L.B. could call me into her office and shut the door to tell me that reading my book changed the way she acts toward her elderly mom, who can drive her bananas. "I thought of you and your mom and realized how lucky I am to have mine around." Her mascara started to run. "So thank you for that," she said. "Thank you."

I wrote so I could sit in a book reading in front of two old friends whom I was astonished to see, whose friendships I'd lost a decade before during those kinds of misunderstandings that go nuclear and leave you shell-shocked, to mix the metaphors of two different World Wars. My book was like shorthand—this is who I was then, and this is who I am now, and maybe we can be friends again. And if not, thank you for showing up, willing to listen.

So I could possess one photo that pretty much makes me fall in love with John every time I look at it. It was taken at my friend Manfred's book soiree. I'm in the foreground, wearing a cobalt silk dress John had made for me in Hong Kong. I'm holding my book in one hand and emphatically gesturing with the other, reveling in performing a reading. I'm blurry, because the camera is focused on my husband. He's off to my side, a little behind me. He's watching me with a tiny smile, with quiet, patient love. He's not reviewing me; he's just happy to witness me in a moment of being fully myself.

A few months after this book came out—long enough to have surfed some waves of euphoria and disappointment—I went to Copenhagen to interview the world-famous chef René Redzepi. He created the restaurant Noma, which has repeatedly been named the best in the world, and he's credited with basically inventing Nordic cuisine. ("Nordic cuisine," in case you're wondering, involves, but is not limited to, live ants that taste like citrus and beets that changed my life.) In short, René's a genius, though he rejects the term. But Noma has not yet been granted three Michelin stars, that Holy Grail for restaurants.

And he essentially told me, "Three stars? Would I like them? Sure, of course. I'd be lying if I said I wouldn't want three Michelin stars. But do I need them? Do they make my food taste better? I have my three stars. They are my three kids."

I thought of my book, my vulnerable little book,

living out there in the world on its own, subject at any time to being slapped with anything from one to five stars from anyone who wants to loathe it or love it. I thought of my two kids, my two little kids, whose existence is certainly more the fulfillment of my dreams than the book I longed to write.

I'm deeply wary of ennobling anything in terms of motherhood, but René's words moved me. He reminded me that I get to go home to my children, who mean so much more than any rave reviews.

I know better than to expect a *thing* to bring me fulfillment (except for a brow lift; seriously, that thing would do it for me), and a book is a thing. But while this book is a product, it is a product of *me*. Its creation asked so much of me that I thought it fair to have expectations of it in return. Yet as much as I love this book, I can't expect it to love me back. When it comes to those who love me back the most, my friend Victoria illuminated the worthiness of my efforts when she uttered these words:

> "You gave your children the story of their mother."

I hadn't thought of it that way until she put it so simply. I did. They have the story of me, about not just the mother, but the *person* they've made of me. Inside that story is the story of them—how deeply they were longed for, and how much they are treasured. I'm helping my kids compose their stories just as they shape mine. When I think of all the things I'll never know about my mom, I daresay I feel like I've given my children a gift of all the things they may (or desperately may not) want to know about me.

Around the same time, I came across a recording of the Beat poet Allen Ginsberg in which he declares, "Wanting approval is a kind of aggression." He characterizes it as a petitioning—and fundamentally, a demand.

To me, the vulnerability of wanting approval, the shared human-ness of the appeal, and the honesty of appreciating it deeply mitigates any of its aggressiveness. But his words kept disturbing me. I couldn't put them to rest. Why? Either they were true or they were not—why were they dogging me? And I finally realized his accusation of aggression rang true, because it's an assault I'd been committing against myself, especially when it came to this book. Did it/I sell enough? Did it/I reach enough people? Do people love it/me?

But those aren't the right questions. These are the right questions:

Did I say what I want to say?

Did I tell my story in a way that is true?

Did the act of writing—of finding *le mot juste*, just the right words to turn my life into stories that could possibly touch people—fulfill me?

As grueling and challenging and occasionally misunderstood as my efforts may be—did my words also entertain, inform, and move someone who didn't think s/he was reading a "trashy romance novel"?

Did I dream of something and achieve it?

Have I given my children answers to questions they don't know to ask yet?

Have I given myself answers to questions I didn't know I had until I wrote myself?

Is this book enough? Because if it's enough that I wrote it, then *I'm* enough. Because I am this story.

And if the answer is yes, then I can walk home peacefully, and I don't need to look for myself outside of myself, in a bookstore window on Broadway, or in anyone else's reflection.

Have a Coke Cake and a Smile

Around the turn of the last century, my great-grandfather, the awesomely named Luther Branch Coley, worked as the assistant manager of the Atlantic Ice and Coal Company of Atlanta. This was back in the day when getting a soft drink necessitated a visit to a soda fountain, where your beverage would be served by a jerk. Young Luther thus had reason to know one Asa Candler fairly well. Mr. Candler happened to own a little enterprise called The Coca-Cola Company, and he advised my great-grandfather to buy some shares—as many as he could. Luther rustled up some cash, and his investment in Coca-Cola meant that his son, my grandfather, grew up comfortably and caffeinated. My grandfather, Marion Hull Coley, cofounded the Coca-Cola Bottling Company of Cape Cod. He kept his Coke stock, did just fine, and passed it on to my mom and his other four kids. This meant a couple of things:

- A bunch of Coleys (Faith Coley Salie, included) were able to afford to go to college. This is why any reports of Coca-Cola causing diabetes or stripping paint off cars leaves me unmoved. You know what Coke causes? Bills to be paid.

- We were never allowed to drink Pepsi or a Pepsi product. I was probably the only eight-year-old who cared about the difference between 7Up and Sprite or who, despite the disparity in their honorifics, could argue for the superiority of Mr. Pibb over Dr Pepper. We patronized McDonald's, but not Burger King, because the former served the family nectar and the latter served the liquid of the Dark Side. Your taste buds don't have to be too evolved to discern the difference between crap and goodness, and I can remember at least one time my father ushered us all out of a restaurant when a waiter tried to pass off Pepsi as The Real Thing.

It also meant cake.

Coke cake was just something we had every once in a while—a normal part of the homemade dessert rotation my mom always provided. I didn't even realize it was unusual to feature America's finest soft drink in a baked good until I left for college and mentioned it, and people would gasp, "*Coke* cake? What is that?!!" Followed by either, "Does it really have Coke in it?" Or the rarer but hopeful, "Does it have cocaine in it?"

It would be irresponsible of me not to warn you about the Curse of the Coke Cake. Simply put: do not let Coca-Cola cake anywhere near your wedding. My brother David created the most stunning four story Coke cake for his sister-in-law Nicole's wedding with raspberry preserve filling and a fondant icing that would make Martha Stewart's meringues weep. For my first marriage, he baked three elegant tiers of it for my engagement party, which he decorated with fresh flowers. I was married in Scotland for my practice wedding and even had an extremely perplexed local bakery make Coca-Cola "fairy cakes"* for the rehearsal dinner party.

Nicole got divorced. So did I. Let this be a lesson to you. Coke cake knows. It knows The Real Thing when it comes to love and will tank shitty marriages.

I believe this cake wants to live as a bundt. My brother loves offering it as a sheet cake, but we all know about the devastation he's wrought through his baking. There's something both sturdy and elegant about the bundt, and you can't beat the way the warm and thick Coke frosting cascades over the sides.

So here's my mom's recipe. If the word "moist" makes you uncomfortable, then don't try this at home. As you know, I always triple the vanilla extract and probably add too many miniature marshmallows, because life can only be made better by pillows of corn syrup. Please enjoy and think of Gail.

---

* "Fairy cakes" are what they call cupcakes in the UK. "Fairy cakes" is also my safe word.

GAIL'S COCA-COLA CAKE

2 sticks butter (salted—what are you crazy, using
   unsalted??)
1½ cups mini marshmallows
3 heaping tablespoons cocoa powder
1 cup Coke
2 cups sugar
2 cups flour, plus extra for dusting
2 large eggs
½ cup buttermilk
1 teaspoon baking soda
1 teaspoon vanilla extract

Preheat the oven to 350°F.

In a saucepan, on medium-high heat, melt the butter with the marshmallows, cocoa powder, and Coke, stirring it until it boils. Then remove it from the heat. In a mixing bowl, pour the cocoa mixture over the sugar and flour and beat until combined, about 1 minute. Add the eggs and mix until combined.

In a separate bowl, whisk the buttermilk, baking soda, and vanilla extract (I use 3 teaspoons). Pour the buttermilk mixture into the batter and beat for about 1 minute.

Pour the cake batter into a greased and floured bundt pan. (I use Baker's Joy. If you use two 6 cups bundt pans ((like I do)), then bake for 30 to 35 minutes.) If you use the normal large 12 cups bundt pan, then bake for 50 to 55 minutes, or until a toothpick inserted in the center comes out clean. Allow the cake to cool for 10 minutes, then flip it onto a cooling rack.

For the frosting:

1 stick butter
5 to 6 tablespoons Coke
2 heaping tablespoons cocoa powder
1 box confectioner's sugar

In a saucepan over low to medium heat, combine the butter, Coke, and cocoa powder and melt until just boiling, stirring often so the cocoa powder doesn't burn. Pour the mixture over the confectioner's sugar and beat with mixer until smooth.

Pour the frosting over the bundt cake.

Enjoy!

*HAVE
A COKE CAKE
AND
A SMILE*

277

Approval Junkie
Discussion Questions

1. Faith begins her memoir with this epigraph by Samuel Beckett: "Fail again. Fail better." How does it reflect the theme of the book?

2. When it comes to seeking approval, are you more of a Kanye West or a Sally Field? Do you think it's "a hunger" that we should try to "transcend"?

3. In "Howler Monkey," Faith writes about the "exhausting psychic noogies" of her wasband's nicknames for her. What did they reveal about their relationship, and why do you think she endured his hazing for so long? Have you ever found yourself in a similar situation? When did you realize it was time to move on?

5. In "Miss Aphrodite," Faith writes about the year she won her high school pageant, which was also the year she didn't become valedictorian, didn't get asked to prom, and didn't eat a satisfying meal. In high school, what goals did you prioritize? Have your values changed since then? How?

6. Faith lists a few questions she'd ask her mother—if

she could—in "Extra Vanilla." What are the top three questions you'd like to ask your mother? If she's alive, what keeps you from asking? Faith suggests, "You may not really consider how much you're like your mom if she's still around." Is this true for you? How are you like your mother, and do you embrace the similarities?

7. In "The Best Hand Job Ever," Faith writes, "Seems to me there are a couple ways to win approval when it comes to sex: one is through having it lots of different ways and the other is by not having it at all." Do you agree, and do you think most women feel constrained by this notion?

8. In "Face for Radio," Faith shares the listening skills she's learned as a radio host. What does she think makes a good listener? What are your own best and worst tendencies as a listener? What's the question you're longing to ask—and of whom?

9. Faith explores her relationship to anger in "Shrink Rapt." How do you express anger? How were you taught to get "bull tinky"? Have you ever been in therapy? What's the most useful wisdom you've gleaned from a therapist?

10. At the end of "What I Wore to My Divorce," Faith imagines talking to her former, sadder self and comforting her about how her life will turn out. If you could sit on the bed beside a younger you, what would you tell her?

11. When you're in a relationship, do you care who says I love you first? What did you make of Faith's hurling of a "love boomerang"? Have you ever done the same?

12. Have you ever "peed on a storybook moment"?

13. As a panelist on *Wait Wait . . . Don't Tell Me!*, Faith learned that spontaneity trumps preparation. Do you think this holds true in other arenas? Which approach do you favor in your own life?

14. Faith confesses her addiction to eyelash extensions in "On the Fringe: A Cautionary Tale." What lengths have you gone to in order to feel pretty? Do you regret anything, or do you agree with Oscar Wilde that "It is only the shallow people who do not judge by appearances"?

15. "My Husband's Dog Is Not My Kids' Brother" addresses the perils of expressing one's opinion, especially if you're a woman, and especially online. Have you ever dealt with personal attacks on social media? How do you deal with them—do you attack back with CAPS LOCK or ignore them?

16. Why do you believe Faith is so intent on breastfeeding her second child? Why does she call the process "both miraculous and brutal"? Do you agree that it's a good metaphor for parenthood?

17. In what ways does Faith seek the approval of others? In what ways does she seek her own approval? Are both pursuits of value?

18. Faith dedicates the book's last essay to her daughter and not her son because, she writes, there are "a million more ways for a woman to gain or lose approval than a man." What are some examples?

19. In your opinion, has Faith's lifelong need for approval been a help or a hindrance?